I N V E S T I G A Ç Ã O

I|U

COEDITION

Imprensa da Universidade de Coimbra
Email: imprensa@uc.pt
URL: http//www.uc.pt/imprensa_uc
Vendas online: http://livrariadaimprensa.uc.pt
UNINT University Press

EDITORIAL COORDINATION

Imprensa da Universidade de Coimbra

GRAPHIC DESIGN

Imprensa da Universidade de Coimbra

TRANSLATION

Sílvia Ferreira

TRANSLATION REVIEW

Mick Greer

COVER IMAGE

Aerial view of the Paço das Escolas with the Joanine Library on the left
© Nuno Antunes

INFOGRAPHICS

Mickael Silva

ISBN

978-989-26-2632-1

ISBN DIGITAL

978-989-26-2633-8

DOI

https://doi.org/10.14195/978-989-26-2633-8

SUPPORT

This work is financed by National Funds through FCT - Fundação para a Ciência e a Tecnologia, I.P., under the project UIDB/00417/2020

KING JOHN V LIBRARY AT COIMBRA

HISTORY AND CONSTRUCTION, ARCHITECTURE AND ART

ROBERT C. SMITH

Critical edition by Sílvia Ferreira

INDEX

On the Importance of Knowing How to See

Robert C. Smith, the American art historian and author of the *work* whose critical edition is now presented, was certainly not a secondary figure: neither in his native USA nor, much less, in the environment of what we can conveniently refer to as the Portuguese historiography of the specialty—where he would stand out as a star, illuminating areas of intense obscurity, which makes his work, decades later, the foundation upon which future generations continue to build their own contributions.

Equipped with a high degree of specialized training (which distinguished him from the empiricism that essentially dominated the national historical-artistic practices at the time), his qualities as an indefatigable worker would generally make him the first explorer of each new territory. This was indeed the case in the studies he dedicated to Nicolau Nasoni, André Soares, or Frei José de Santo António Ferreira Vilaça, to the gilded woodwork of the altars (and churches) of the metropolis, or to its expansion across the Atlantic, within the framework of the so-called Luso-Brazilian Baroque: all of these were discoveries of a personality with whom, in fact, Portugal and its artistic heritage would incur a debt that was never truly settled.

The same can be said, in fact, about this authentic gem of the Baroque World that represents the University Library of Coimbra, commonly known as the Joanina Library. While it is true that it still awaits the comprehensive study it objectively deserves, once again, Robert Smith would prove to be a pioneer in this matter. His untimely death would indeed interrupt the publication of a book, the *original* of which would be preserved for nearly half a century in the Art Archive of the Calouste Gulbenkian Foundation, which the historian had designated as the heir to his working documents.

It was to the publication of this *work* that Sílvia Ferreira turned her attention, equipped with familiarity with the subject and the respective author, as well as the competence that is universally recognized in her: thus, putting an end to half a century of speculation. Hence, the refined interest and natural expectation with which the publication of the mythical text about this fascinating building would be awaited: an expectation that this current work does not disappoint—instead, it helps to fill a gap (while dispelling the legend or myth of an unpublished book ready for publication), within the framework of an exhaustive endeavour that explores, to the fullest extent possible, the available sources.

In fact, the *original* in question does not exactly constitute a *text*, albeit unfinished, to which the title of a *book* could be given under any circumstances. Rather, it consists of (at least) three typewritten copies of what can be considered the final phase of the work to which Smith dedicated his last years (or, at least, his final versions), with the added complication that one is written in Portuguese and the others in English, in addition to presenting significant differences among themselves.

To these, however, one must add a myriad of other sources: a vast volume of "typewritten texts, manuscripts, letters, drawings, photocopies, and more extensive or brief notes on the Joanina Library" (as the author mentions in the extensive *Introduction* that precedes the work), which also intersects in order to not only stabilize the text but also refine the very essence of a thought whose thread his sudden death would cut.

Therefore, whether for the objective utility of understanding the historian's thoughts on one of the most significant national edifices of all time, or, more specifically, for the truly exhaustive work of this critical edition, systematically crossing all available sources, in a narrative enriched by the scientific production generated in the meantime — a fine work that absolutely duplicates the content of the work and the relevance of current access to the materials produced by Smith —, everything in this truly exemplary work by Sílvia Ferreira converges to transform it, henceforth, into a central piece in the bibliography of baroque art, not only nationally but also (given the relevance of the subject matter) internationally.

Indeed, while the Portuguese text primarily focuses on the *History and Construction* of the splendid building (as inferred from its title), supported by documentation preserved in the university archive — also seeking to advance the biographies of the artists and craftsmen involved (such as Gaspar Ferreira, the master builder, and Manuel da Silva, the painter of the shelves, or the duo responsible for the illusionistic *quadrattura* of the ceilings, António Simões Ribeiro and Vicente Nunes) — the chapters written in English aim, through parallel paths, to address the central question, regarding which University sources are completely silent: that of the authorship of the architectural plan of the splendid building. The puzzling enigma of this "Library without an author," as Sílvia Ferreira refers to it, would indeed become the obsidian theme of its last years, anticipated in the very Introduction to the Portuguese text, where he will initially present arguments in favour of his thesis (even if deferring its greater development to a future plan — "as I shall show in due course," he would state — precisely that of the English version of his text): that of the authorship of Claude de Laprade (Avignon, 1682 – Lisbon, 1738) regarding the plans of the Joanina. He will thus be, for the American historian, the missing author of the Library.

And it is, in fact, in the service of this search that we can gather the *best Smith*: the one that reminds us of the precocious author of the extraordinary text "João Frederico Ludovice, an eighteenth-century architect in Portugal", published in 1936 — a very important synthesis of his doctoral dissertation defended at Harvard in the same year, which likewise awaits the much-needed (critical) edition in Portuguese. Just as then, the remarkable research he is now conducting, in the strictly formal realm that is his (the "stylistic analysis is one of the purposes of this book" he will write in the aforementioned *Introduction*), intersects with a systematic survey of the contemporary international aesthetic reality (including the respective iconographic sources), placing him in an absolutely unique position within the Portuguese academic universe.

It is in his light (far beyond the strict positivism that was sought to be attached to him) that he ultimately draws his conclusions: the most correct, in fact, and well-founded that historiographical criticism allows to elaborate. Far from all empiricism, it is in the exercise of the strictest scientific rigor that his ability to *know how to see* is grounded.

Hence that *insightful gaze*[1] which, as a rule, would effectively allow him to see far and, especially, with singular anticipation: as would happen with Ludovice's role in Mafra — or, in between, with his accurate intuition regarding the authorship of Antonio Canevari concerning the Coimbra university tower, which he would mention in these very pages[2] — as is now the case with Claude de Laprade and the Coimbra University Library. The importance of *knowing*

---

[1] PIMENTEL, António Filipe, "Um olhar perspicaz: Robert Smith e o Monumento de Mafra", in *Robert C. Smith (1912-1975). A investigação na História de Arte*, Lisboa, Fundação Calouste Gulbenkian, 2000, Cat., p. 277-287.

[2] Cfr. I*dem*, "António Canevari e a torre da Universidade de Coimbra", in Natália Marinho Ferreira Alves (coord), *Artistas e Artífices e a sua mobilidade no mundo de expressão portuguesa: actas do VII Colóquio Luso-Brasileiro de História da Arte*, Porto, 2005, pp. 49-58.

how to see, illustrated in a masterful lesson of historiography, whose current utility seems undeniable.

It is, in fact, about a truncated dream: witnessed in the triple version (unfinished) of the text that was to structure the great book on the University Library, a comprehensive study that death prevented him from completing, and in the multiple notes that would support it, all integrated into the legacy of his scientific estate, which the historian would leave, in his last wishes, to the Foundation that so supported his projects. But it is also about another dream, happily fulfilled: that of the publication of these texts, with possible standardization, thanks to the extreme diligence carried out by Silvia Ferreira, who successfully managed to integrate everything.

Effectively, through her diligent work in patient archaeology, not only is the author's thought returned to us (accompanied, step by step, by the respective critical fortune), but also, in the process, an extensive and important biographical note about the remarkable American art historian is established, which is essential for an integrated understanding of his own professional activity. In fact, by collecting and expanding the data presented, it goes back a quarter of a century, in the first and only systematic attention that would be dedicated to him — in the important exhibition[3] organized in the wake of the privileged relationship he maintained with the Calouste Gulbenkian Foundation and the aforementioned incorporation of his documentary collection into its Art Archive — the work of Sílvia Ferreira (condensed in the splendid *Introduction* to the volume, within the section dedicated to "The Author") finally enables a broad and systematic view of his personal journey. From his formative years (and early contact with the Portuguese artistic reality — notably with Mafra and Coimbra — justifying his peculiar

[3] Robert C. Smith (1912-1975). A investigação na História de Arte, Lisboa, Fundação Calouste Gulbenkian, 2000, Cat.

professional choice) to the endpoints (and the obsidian project of the Joanina), passing through the intermediates (in which, both in the USA and in Portugal, he would accumulate positions of academic prestige, simultaneously building a dense network of interrelations that would become a powerful operational aid), he was never, objectively, a *secondary figure*: neither in his country of origin nor, much less, in what he would adopt as his research territory. This would make all the difference...

It is certain that, if the extraordinary Coimbra University Library has not yet received, through this means, the synthesis work, the *comprehensive study* that Robert Smith somehow envisioned (focused, as it obviously would be, on the problems of "stylistic analysis," objectively assumed as "one of the purposes of this book"), the astonishing work of Sílvia Ferreira — an exhaustive inventory of the subsequent historiographical production related to these subjects — brings her very close to that final goal, transforming into a *book* what was, in fact, merely the raw material for such an objective: and, at the same time, contributing to settle the enormous debt that Portugal and its artistic heritage would incur with the historian.

In this sense, as I note here a few lines of introduction to this remarkable work — a double *magnum opus*, after all — I feel the weight of folly: whether due to the prestigious aura surrounding the illustrious memory of its author, or the already established career of the author of this most notable edition. Personally, I can only commend the timely publication of this extremely important text by the great historian (which will only be criticized for its lateness), and especially the just association promoted within it between the University of Coimbra and the Calouste Gulbenkian Foundation: not, of course, because that is my *alma mater* and this is the institution I currently serve (even if such circumstances may weigh on my particular affections), but for the obvious reasons that arise, on one hand, from the expectation with which, in the years immediately preceding his premature death, this study and its conclusions would have been eagerly awaited at the old Coimbra University, and to feed the author's justified hope that the Foundation would be its potential publisher (as inferred from the second chapter, now published). Today, with the roles reversed (the University lent the presses, to which the Foundation is associated, thus enabling the endeavour), not everything, in fact, would be disadvantages in this belated edition of the drafts left unfinished by Robert C. Smith. In the nearly five decades that separate us from its production, not only has the historiography of Portuguese art evolved, allowing for advancements that, as usual, would endorse the pioneering vision of the American historian, but (by that very means) would provide the grand undertaking of critical edition with a breadth of material that ensures the historian's contribution is inscribed in a fundamentally dense fabric of knowledge — thus enabling Sílvia Ferreira to carry out her fruitful work with the sophisticated detail that transforms it not only into a model but, very especially, into a powerful instrument for the dissemination of studies on Baroque art in Portugal and, generically, on what has come to be known as *the art of libraries* — and, within it, that extraordinary jewel of universal artistic heritage that is commonly referred to as the Biblioteca Joanina. And it will be all of this, ultimately, that will matter *to know how to see* today.

Lisbon, July 31, 2024.

António Filipe Pimentel

Getting to Know Joanina

In 2024, the "Joanina Digital" project was launched, funded by the Emirate of Sharjah, with the aim of digitizing the entire collection of the Noble Floor of the Joanina Library (approximately 30,000 volumes) by 2029. A recent survey of the interior and exterior of the building was also conducted using 3D laser scanning techniques for a virtual modelling of Joanina. Both initiatives testify to the importance of Joanina as a historical construction and cultural heritage, which we must continue to learn about and preserve. This knowledge is complemented by research on the Library as a system of organizing bibliographic information and on the Library as an architectural and artistic creation. It involves revisiting the collection and the building with the critical perspective provided by computing.

Studies on the Joanina Library are an integral part of its self-knowledge at a time when digitization changes our view of its legacy and expands its modes of presence in our imagination and research practices. The critical edition of *King John V Library at Coimbra. History and construction. Architecture and art*, edited by Sílvia Ferreira, makes accessible a work that was previously only available in typescript in the author's estate donated to the Calouste Gulbenkian Foundation. Dedicated to the history of the building's construction and the stylistic analysis of its artistic elements, Robert C. Smith's work represented a significant advancement in knowledge at the time, particularly due to its systematic documentary research and the integrated analysis it proposes, as noted in the introductory study. Therefore, it is an invaluable contribution to the bibliography on Joanina that we must highlight.

Manuel Portela
Director of the General Library of the University of Coimbra

INTRODUCTION

Prefatory note

This critical edition of the unpublished work of Robert C. Smith (1912-1975) on the Joanina Library in Coimbra was financed by National Funds through FCT - Fundação para a Ciência e a Tecnologia, I.P. It has been carried out within the scope of the IHA seed project "The Joanina Library in Coimbra, history and art. An unpublished study by Robert C. Smith" and financed by National Funds through FCT- Fundação para a Ciência e a Tecnologia, IP, in the scope of the project (UIDB/00417/2020), https://doi.org/10.54499/UIDB/00417/2020. It was developed in collaboration with the Coimbra University Press and the Calouste Gulbenkian Foundation.

Editorial options

Robert C. Smith's unpublished work on the history and art of the Joanina Library in Coimbra is part of his estate bequeathed to the Calouste Gulbenkian Foundation. It consists of three typed manuscripts, one written in Portuguese and the other two in English, which I consider the final versions of his work[1]. The first is entitled *História*

[1] There is another copy of the chapter entitled *História e Construção*, which is also written in Portuguese but is less complete in terms of the author's notes.

e Construção (History and Construction) and essentially concerns the construction process of the Library, especially the works and the artists who worked on it. The second version is written in English, as well as the notes to the text, which are in a separate document. The English version is a systematic stylistic analysis of the façade and interiors of the library, through which Smith tries to discover the artist responsible for the Library's conception. Smith compares the doorway and interiors of the monument with Italian and French Baroque and analyses the stone works executed by the Avignon sculptor Claude Laprade, whether for the University of Coimbra, the tomb of Vista Alegre, in Ílhavo, or the doorways of the Church of Senhor das Barrocas, in Aveiro, which he attributes to him. After these comparisons, Smith's best guess as to who designed the sumptuous monument in João V's reign is the sculptor, Claude Laprade.

Given the way the documents were presented, with the first chapter written in Portuguese and the second in English, a bilingual edition was chosen. This option presents a work that could also be enjoyed by an international public, as it more widely disseminates the constructive history of the Joanina Library and the stylistic analysis of its architecture and applied arts, as well as systematising knowledge about this building, its stylistic predecessors and others that succeeded it.

The dispersion and volume of typescripts, manuscripts, letters, drawings, photocopies and longer or shorter notes on the Joanina Library in Robert C. Smith's collection required slow and meticulous work in organising and comparing the information contained in them with the texts of the two typescript chapters and notes of the unpublished work. It turned out that almost all the information he had accurately compiled by means of worksheets, notes, handwritten and typewritten transcriptions of contracts, payment lists for artists and other workers on the Library, extracts from printed works and studies, is mirrored in the two chapters he wrote on the Joanina.

Bearing in mind that they were at different stages of completion and that the final revisions had not yet been made, the following options were taken by us in the present edition of Robert C. Smith's manuscripts and typed texts:

1) The form and content of the original texts have been respected, with the few spelling and grammatical mistakes in the Portuguese version corrected. This follows a practice described in letters and other documents, which prove that the author often delegated this mission to his friends and colleagues, especially Flávio Gonçalves and his most frequently chosen editor, Rogério Moura, among others[2] .
2) I have chosen to integrate the annotations that the original texts contained in the final text; such as substitution of words, insertion of footnotes or references to matters addressed elsewhere in the book. Robert C. Smith would have added all these annotations and, in order not to overload the final version with notes, which would disrupt its reading, it was decided to absorb all the author's annotations in the text.
3) The spelling at the time of writing and the citation rules of the original notes and bibliography have been maintained.
4) Incomplete or missing information in some notes of the original texts was added, namely references to documental sources,

---

[2] In the epistolography exchanged with Flávio Gonçalves, there were frequent references to his friend's amendments to his texts. Let's take two letters from Robert C. Smith to Flávio Gonçalves as examples. The first one is dated 19th June 1971, from Pennsylvania, and states: "I have read with the greatest attention, word for word, the text of my article on Matias de Lis de Miranda. I thank you very much for the extreme care you exercised over my choice of words and at the same time I apologise for two horrendous grammatical mistakes I made, besides the entirely incomplete sentence I left in the original." In the other, dated 26th June of the same year and, again, from Pennsylvania, Smith underlines his gratitude: "I thank you for your kindness in completing the bibliography of *ex-votos* for my respective article, in whose notes I have already put it". Municipal Library Rocha Peixoto (MLRP). *Flávio Gonçalves estate. Letters by Robert C. Smith.*

such as the Coimbra University General Library Archive and the Joanina Library Archive. Besides these, there were bibliographical references to Studies that sometimes only mentioned the author's last name, accompanied by a date or not, and the number of pages.

5) I have chosen to present my additions to the original text in a different colour, which will allow readers to see what is original in Robert C. Smith's text, and what I have added.
6) Footnotes have been included, especially in the case of passages in the text that are less clear or refer to updated bibliography on the themes dealt with by the author in that specific passage of his text.

Presentation

The author - brief notes

Robert C. Smith was born in the United States of America in Crawford, New Jersey, on 26th February 1912. An only child, coming from a family of the American upper middle class, he travelled as a teenager with his parents through several European countries, including Spain and Portugal. This European tour, common among some wealthy American families of the time, fed his already latent curiosity for the arts and predisposed him to an informed worldview, which he cultivated throughout his life. His entry into the Fine Arts course at Harvard University in Boston in 1929, at the age of 17, certainly reflected this recent intellectual stimulation.

Robert C. Smith's first contacts with Portuguese Baroque art or art executed for Portugal began with his trip to Naples in 1932 to study the art of the southern Italian Peninsula. The discovery in the

Palatine Library of the Regia di Caserta of drawings executed by the Neapolitan architect Luigi Vanvitelli for the Chapel of St. John the Baptist in the Church of St. Roque in Lisbon, commissioned by King João V (1707-1750) in 1742, directed his studies towards Portugal. In 1933, he obtained a Bachelor of Arts degree summa cum laude and in 1934 a Master's degree with a dissertation entitled "The minor architect Luigi Vanvitelli". Between 1934 and 1935, he travelled to Portugal and visited Lisbon, Mafra and Coimbra. It was during his stay in Mafra that he became aware of the importance of the Nossa Senhora and Santo António de Mafra Palace-Convent. The building and its architect, Frederico Ludovice, aroused his interest and led him to his doctoral subject. A summary of his thesis was published under the title "João Frederico Ludovice, an eighteenth century architect in Portugal" in *The Art Bulletin* (Vol. 18, no. 3rd Sept. 1936, pp. 273-370), a journal of the College Art Association of America. This choice was indeed very particular, considering that he was an American art historian in the 1930s, a decade in which interest in Iberian-American art was not common among his peers. However, the decision can be explained both by Smith's interests and by the teaching method practised and developed at Harvard University in Boston. In fact, this art historian belonged to the group of scholars of Latin American culture at that university and other institutions devoted to the subject. As early as 1936, the year his doctoral thesis was finished, he started collaborating on the *Handbook of Latin American Studies*, published by the Hispanic Division, based at the Library of Congress in Washington. Smith was responsible for the section on the art and culture of Brazil, a collaboration that would only end in 1962. His trip to Minas Gerais, Brazil, in 1937, to study colonial baroque art inevitably led him to Portugal, these artistic expressions' country of origin. Between 1939 and 1942, he was co-director of the Hispanic Division, directing and curating the prints and photographic section between 1942 and 1943. He was also co-editor, along with Elizabeth Wilder, of *A Guide to the Art of Latin America* (1948) published by the Library of Congress. He compiled and arranged material for lectures by American colleagues on Brazilian colonial art and collected some 10 000 photographs for the photographic archive of the Hispanic Division. Pursuing his vocation for Iberoamerican studies, in 1949 he chaired the Inter-American Studies Committee of the University of Pennsylvania.

Between 1937 and 1939, he taught at the University of Illinois and, between 1945 and 1946, at Sweet Briar College, finishing his academic career at the School of Fine Arts of the University of Pennsylvania, which began in 1947 and ended in 1972 due to disability retirement. He devoted himself essentially to the teaching of Ibero-American art and architecture, as well as that of North America[3].

His visits to Portugal intensified following the invitation he received from the Portuguese embassy in Washington to join the Commission of official representatives of the United States at the Commemorations of the Double Centennial of 1940. In February, the Portuguese Ambassador to the United States, António de Bianchi received a letter from António Oliveira Salazar, President of the Council of Ministers, urging that the ambassadors of countries with whom Portugal had friendly relations and cultural proximity were officially invited to send their representatives to participate in the double centenary event. The invitation was immediately accepted by the United States, which appointed a diplomatic commission to travel to Portugal and take part in the celebrations. The commission was made up of Anthony J. Drexel Biddle Jr., US Ambassador to Poland; Charles Edward Courtney, representing the US Navy;

---

[3] On Robert C. Smith's training, working methods and vocation for Iberoamerican studies, see Wohl, H. (2000). Robert C. Smith e a História da Arte nos Estados Unidos. In Jorge R. and Manuel C. (eds.). *Robert C. Smith. A investigação em história de arte* (pp. 17-29). Calouste Gulbenkian Foundation and Russel-Wood, A.J.R. (2000). Robert Chester Smith: researcher and historian (...) (pp. 31-65). In *ibidem*.

Paul T. Culbertson, from the Department of Foreign Affairs and Robert C. Smith, representing the Hispanic Division of the Library of Congress in Washington.

Through this documentation, in the custody of the archive and library of the Diplomatic Institute of the Portuguese Ministry of Foreign Affairs, it is clear that Robert C. Smith was already well known to the Portuguese community in Washington and Philadelphia. His name appears alongside other scholars of Portuguese history, culture and art, natives of the USA or immigrants, such as Manuel Cardoso, an Azorean immigrant in Washington[4].

Many of these historians were initially called upon by the Portuguese Embassy in Washington to collaborate in programmed initiatives mainly aimed at the Portuguese community in the USA, but also as a vehicle for the dissemination and propaganda of Portuguese history and art among the American public. Robert C. Smith was invited to give a series of lectures on Portuguese art, so he wrote to António Ferro requesting images to accompany them. The images requested could not have been more emblematic: Lisbon Cathedral, Jerónimos Monastery, Convent of Christ in Tomar, among others. He essentially asked for examples of 16th and 17th century painting and sculpture[5].

Another recently identified activity by Smith was as a specialist on Portuguese art in the United States, close to his first official visit to Portugal. When the American art historian Georgiana G. King visited Portugal in 1935 with the intention of getting to know and analyse some of the most important medieval Portuguese monuments, she

[4] Almeida, O.T. (2013). Manoel da Silveira Cardozo (1911-1985). Um historiador picoense nos Estados Unidos. *Boletim do Núcleo Cultural da Horta*. 22 123-136. Manuel Silveira Cardoso was director of the Oliveira Lima Library, a lecturer at the Catholic University of Washington and a close contact of Robert C. Smith.

[5] On Robert C. Smith's participation in the 1940 double centenary celebrations, see Ferreira, S. (November 2022). Gold on Blue in Philadelphia. Robert C. Smith and the Installation of the 'Portuguese Chapel' at the Samuel S. Fleisher Art Memorial. *RIHA Journal*.

prepared a notebook, which only a sudden illness prevented her from completing and working on more systematically[6].

This document, known as the *Portuguese Notebook*, was left unfinished and was not published during Georgiana King's lifetime. What is of particular interest to us is that Robert C. Smith was the person contacted to review the manuscript, namely regarding the spelling of certain Portuguese place names and monuments, as well as the relevance and pertinence of publishing his colleague's study.

Always well received in Portugal, especially by the cultural institutions and other places of the regions where he carried out his research, Smith managed to create a network of contacts and influence that greatly contributed to the success of his studies, as made clear by the multiple means by which they were disseminated. From local newspapers like *Comércio do Porto*, *O Tripeiro* (Porto), *Notícias dos Arcos* (Arcos de Valdevez), to scientific journals in Portugal (*Belas-Artes, Bracara Augusta* and *Colóquio Artes*) and abroad (*Apollo, Antiques, The Burlington Magazine* and *The Connoisseur*), as well as prestigious book editions, Smith used everything at his disposal to spread his knowledge of the Portuguese Baroque heritage.

He was a member of, and collaborated with, various cultural institutions, including the Athenaeum of Philadelphia, the American Philosophical Society, the Winterthur Museum and the Colonial Williamsburg Foundation. In Portugal, and at a very early stage, he was admitted to the National Academy of Fine Arts[7] and to the Association of Portuguese Archaeologists[8].

---

[6] The critical edition of this travelogue was recently published by Neto, M.J. (2022). *Arquitetura Medieval Portuguesa. O olhar da americana Georgiana G. King em 1935.* Caleidoscópio.

[7] Proposed by José de Figueiredo as a foreign correspondent member, he was elected on 14th July 1937, and formally admitted on 12th August 1940. National Academy of Fine Art, membership files.

[8] Date of admission form 23rd December 1937, member no. 298, corresponding member. Association of Portuguese Archaeologists, membership files.

State of the art on the Joanina Library of Coimbra

When Robert C. Smith began to research the constructive history of the Library, its commissioners and patrons, artists and their works, he had a wealth of basic, though undeveloped, information about the specific subject he had chosen. On the history of the university, there were already several comprehensive publications, which he cites throughout his text. Similarly, he drew from the pioneering studies of Vergílio Correia and Father Nogueira Gonçalves for the art of the Coimbra region. His first major concern, as always, was to exhaustively collect all the documentary material and studies dedicated to the subject he intended to address. To do so, he counted on the precious help of his well-placed friends and of others who they introduced to him. After this initial gathering, he worked on the documents, transcribing them and extracting their relevant information. While he was making worksheets of the bibliography he was compiling, he went into the field to find out about the possibility of publishing his work, which he had been looking forward to at least since 1969. Undertaking this mission made perfect sense at the time, due to the absence of an integrated study of the history and art of the Joanina Library. Nonetheless, we may ask ourselves, almost fifty years after his death and the interruption of the project, whether the publication of this work resulting from nearly six years of intermittent research is still relevant.

The answer, surely, can only be positive, and is fully justified by the texts he left unpublished; as well as the work process he undertook, which is well demonstrated by the accessory documentation in his estate.

After Smith's death in 1975, his will made the Calouste Gulbenkian Foundation the trustee of his entire professional estate. Once Smith's legacy had been collected in the United States, these materials remained virtually untouched until the Foundation dedicated a major exhibition to the American professor and historian in 2000[9]. At that time, a group of specialists from different areas of Portuguese and Brazilian history and art history had access to the documents and the potential of that material was rediscovered. Flávio Gonçalves and Helmut Wohl knew it very well, having been sent to the United States to accompany the estate to Portugal.

Due to Smith's full and multifaceted professional life, both in the United States and Brazil, as well as in Portugal and several other European countries to which he travelled for work, the 2000 exhibition and catalogue necessarily had to circumscribe themes and working materials. The unpublished works Smith left behind were identified and some were commented on and studied. However, despite this awareness and the works' importance, the 2000 exhibition and catalogue did not lead to a study project and work on the American historian's life and work.

Only in 2016, in the pursuit of my post-doctoral studies, did I have access to the documentation of this collection. A systematic approach was begun, looking for manuscripts and worksheets that could still answer some questions about the study of Portuguese Baroque woodcarving *in situ* or displaced. As part of this work, I came across the manuscripts and typescripts relating to the publishing project on the Joanina Library of Coimbra. I immediately understood the scope of the research that was involved: systematic bibliographic and archival work, strenuous and disciplined efforts to find the right people to help him with such diverse matters, such as access to the material; Latinists to interpret the inscriptions in the Library; and architects to help reconstruct the plans, not only of the Library, but also of other monuments that were affiliated with it, such as the architect Tasso de Sousa, who worked with him on several occasions to produce plans and drawings.

---

[9] Cf. Jorge R. e Manuel C. (eds.). (2000) - *Robert C. Smith (1912-1975). A investigação em história de arte* (...).

As if all this systematic work, translated into chapters, were not enough, I would soon realise that the King João Library building in Coimbra, its architectural prospectus and interior decoration had never been subject to a comprehensive study of the type that Smith had dedicated to it.

In recent years, the Joanina Library has been the subject of various publications, almost all of them in the context of divulging its factual history; its vast and rich bibliographical collection; its coexistence with the other institutions of the University; the impact it suffered with the Pombaline reform of the *Gerais* and, finally, its place in the pantheon of the world's richest and most beautiful libraries. Within these publications, but also in autonomous writings, it has been the art historian António Filipe Pimentel who has devoted most attention to the art present in its interiors. Based on what was already known and other information that he has identified about the artists and their work in the Library at the time it was built, Pimentel has highlighted the historical and cultural context of its commissioning and production. He rightly emphasises the courtly ambience of the Joanina Library's interiors, in the context of the reign of King João V and its tendency to be international.

António Filipe Pimentel's reading of the significance of the Library as a showcase and enthronement of a way of being a nation and a sovereign (King João V) at that time was not one of Robert C. Smith's interests. These finer, more relational analyses of the spirit of the times in Portugal and in the European countries with which it compared itself were not in his immediate horizons. His method, which some classify as positivist, looked at the object, although with a perfect notion of its context, as something to be deciphered first by observation and then by documentation supported by bibliographical and archival sources. We must not forget that Robert C. Smith mainly investigated and studied monuments and art objects that had not undergone any previous scientific and systematic research. His starting point was often from almost zero.

The research and production process

Robert C. Smith's *modus operandi* for researching and publishing his work is fully mirrored in his King João Library research. From his privileged contacts with the Library's director at the time, Professor Guilherme Braga da Cruz; with other academics, such as Maria Helena da Rocha Pereira; with archivists, such as Dr Lígia Brandão; with publishers, like Livros Horizonte, with institutions, such as the Calouste Gulbenkian Foundation in the person of its president and directors of departments, especially the Fine Arts department; to his colleagues in Portugal and abroad, Smith imposed a dynamic flow that the documentation in his collection illuminated.

There is handwritten and typewritten documentation relating to the history and art of the Joanina Library. However, it is the letters exchanged with numerous personalities in Portugal and abroad that tell us most about the origin of this study project, its lines of research, successes and disappointments, advances and setbacks. In fact, the letters exchanged between Robert C. Smith and Flávio Gonçalves, Egídio Guimarães, Guilherme Braga da Cruz, Maria Helena da Rocha Pereira, Manuel Lopes de Almeida, Yves Bottineau, Germain Bazin and Nuno Tasso de Sousa allow us a better understanding of the birth and evolution of this project that Robert C. Smith cherished until his death.

What the epistolography tells us: the backstage of an investigation

In addition to the handwritten and typewritten documentation concerning the history and art of the library, it is the letters exchanged with numerous personalities in Portugal and abroad that tell us most about the origin of this study project.

The working process of Robert C. Smith, a foreign art historian who was formally received in Portugal for the first time as a member of the United States' delegation at the Portuguese World Exhibition of 1940, relied heavily on the network of contacts he established and expanded over the years he travelled to Portugal.

The final product of the books and articles he published on Portuguese art, in Portugal and abroad, do not allow a glimpse of the long research processes, the *démarches* he carried out with academics, museum directors, government members, public and private institutions, families and friends. Only the reading and analysing of the highly extensive epistolography, which he left scattered throughout all these contacts, could provide a better picture of Smith's *modus operandi* and how it was fundamental to the research he undertook, the lectures and courses he attended and the work he published.

The letters now accessed that refer specifically to his Joanina Library research, particularly those exchanged with his closest interlocutor and friend, Flávio Gonçalves (Professor at the Faculty of Fine Arts in Porto); Alexandre Alves (director of the journal *Beira-Alta*); Egídio Guimarães (director of the Braga Public Library and of the journal *Bracara Augusta*); Nuno Tasso de Sousa[10] (architect); Lígia Brandão (archivist of the Coimbra University Library); Guilherme Braga da Cruz (director of the Coimbra University Library) and Maria Helena da Rocha Pereira (vice-rector of the University of Coimbra) are revealing. They show the hidden face of a long and troubled

[10] Nuno Tasso de Sousa began working with Robert C. Smith when he was still a student at the Faculty of Architecture in Porto. This collaboration resulted in various drawings and plans that the architect used to illustrate several of Smith's publications. These contacts and collaborations lasted until the American art historian's death in 1975. I would like to express my gratitude to Nuno Tasso de Sousa for his generosity in collaborating on the publication of this book and other projects to do with Robert C. Smith's work, including making available the letters exchanged with him and the lively conversations we had in Porto.

process that, in the years of greater investment on his part, was frenetic and passionate. The Library without an architect intrigued him, and his greatest investment in this study lay precisely in trying to affiliate it. How could it be explained that such a monumental undertaking, commissioned by the king, which took around 10 years to complete, involving considerable sums of money, technical and logistical resources, workers from various trades and artists, could remain, almost 250 years after its construction, without its creative soul being known?

Following Robert C. Smith's references to his study of the Joanina Library chronologically, the first that comes to mind is mentioned in a letter written in Lisbon to Egídio Guimarães, dated 7th July 1969. After having mentioned several projects he was working on, Smith says that he delivered the materials for the publication of the book on Marceliano de Araújo[11] and highlights his stay in Coimbra to start his studies on the *Real Livraria*. [12]

The next letter on this theme is much more assertive and informative, although written in an almost telegraphic style. It is addressed to Flávio Gonçalves, from Coimbra, on 7th January 1971, and reads as follows:

> "I arrived here at 11.15 yesterday and was immediately welcomed by Mrs. Lígia Brandão, whom Dr Egídio phoned. I can't imagine a more charming or helpful person than this distinguished curator, who showed me everything there is about the University Library. We found a document of the greatest importance, apparently unpublished, in which the ceiling painter, António Simões Ribeiro describes his work (1724) and reveals that the other person

[11] Smith, R. C. (1970) - *Marceliano de Araújo, escultor bracarense*. Nelita Editora.

[12] Letter from Robert Smith to Egídio Guimarães. *Egídio Guimarães estate*. All references to the epistolography exchanged between Egídio Guimarães belonging to his estate and Robert C. Smith were kindly provided by Eduardo Pires de Oliveira.

who came with him from Lisbon was only a gilder (...) I was very well received by Dr Costa Ramalho[13], with whom I will have lunch on the 9th, Lopes de Almeida[14], who tomorrow will show me some documents he has, and Father Avelino de Jesus Costa"[15].

On the 18th of that month, he wrote again to Egídio Guimarães[16], informing him of the visit to Coimbra and thanking him for the phone call he had made, which opened the doors of that city to him. Both the university and its archives were made available, and he was able to see all the known documentation in the Library. He also mentions that Dr Lopes de Almeida let him copy his

---

[13] Smith refers to Américo da Costa Ramalho (1921-2013), who was a full professor at the University of Coimbra, a scholar of Hellenism, Humanism and Latin, "He was a fellow of the Institute of High Culture at Oxford University (1947-1949); a Member of Parliament (1957-1959) (...) "Visiting Professor of Portuguese", at New York University (1959-1962). Between 1975 and 1977, he taught at several Brazilian universities, namely at the Federal University and at the State University of Rio de Janeiro. He was acting Dean of the Faculty of Letters from 21st January 1969 to 30th April 1969 and effective Director from 17th March 1970 to 1974. At the University, he also held the posts of Director of the University Archive (1973), Director of the Institute for Classical Studies, President of the Centre for Classical and Humanistic Studies, Co-founder and President of the Portuguese Association for Classical Studies". Cf. Américo da Costa Ramalho. https://www.uc.pt/bguc/destaques/AmericoCostaRamalho.

[14] Manuel Lopes de Almeida (1900-1980) was a politician and academic linked to the Portuguese *Estado Novo*. In 1940, he was appointed interim Director-General of Higher Education and Fine Arts and Secretary of State for National Education. Between 1961 and 1962, he was Minister of National Education and was also director of the Coimbra General Library from 1945 to 1970. He was a member of the National Commission for the 5th Centenary of the Death of Prince Henry the Navigator and one of those responsible, alongside Idalino Ferreira da Costa Brochado and António Joaquim Dias Dinis, for the publication of the *Monumenta Henricina*. See ALMEIDA, Manuel Lopes de. 1900-1980, university professor and politician. https://archeevo.amap.pt/details?id=75273.

[15] Avelino Jesus da Costa (1908-2000) was a full professor at the University of Coimbra, specialising in palaeography, epigraphy, archivistics and 13th century ecclesiastical history. Cf. Professor Cónego Avelino de Jesus da Costa (1908-2000). (2007). *Revista de História da Sociedade e da Cultura,* 6. Letter from Smith to Flávio Gonçalves. MLRP, *Flávio Gonçalves estate. Epistolography of Robert C. Smith.*

[16] Letter from Robert C. Smith to Egídio Guimarães. *Egídio Guimarães estate.*

transcriptions. He adds: "The Vice-Rector D. Maria Helena da Rocha Pereira personally showed me the rector's quarters, where I found a painted ceiling, which together with one of the Library's documents, totally unpublished, will be a treasure trove for the book I want to dedicate to this building".

On 20th March, Maria Helena da Rocha Pereira writes to Robert C. Smith:

> "In accordance with your request, I am sending you, as a separate item of mail, five plans of the Joanina Library of this University, to serve as a basis for the study you intend to do, in which we are very interested (...) You may rest assured that we will always be pleased to supply you with the data within our reach for the preparation of your studies of Portuguese art, particularly those concerning our University"[17].

This letter was answered on 9th April. Smith thanked the vice-rector for sending the plans of the Joanina Library and extended his question and curiosity to the coat of arms painted on the sacristy of the Church of Santo António dos Olivais in Coimbra, a space that he considered artistically parallel to some aspects of the Library:

> "I am pleased to inform you that I have received these items, which are essential for the study I am preparing on the construction and authorship of the library. I look forward to receiving any information you may have on the possibility of identifying the coat of arms painted on the ceiling of the sacristy of the Church of Santo António dos Olivais in Coimbra"[18].

---

[17] Calouste Gulbenkian Foundation (CGF). *The Robert Smith Archive*. Box. 1, doc. 19a.

[18] CGF. *The Robert C. Smith Archive*. Box. 1, doc. 19b.

Early 1971 was a very busy time for Smith's research on the Library. It is clear that he was deeply involved in trying to understand all the details of its construction and interior decoration, which inevitably included its Latin inscriptions and those affixed to the main doorway of the Church of Senhor das Barrocas in Aveiro, where he found affinities with the work of the Library. He writes to Flávio Gonçalves:

> "I will, however, ask you a favour regarding the sheet accompanying this letter. It is about some Latin inscriptions which I translated with the help of two professors from the major seminary. I would like to know (1) if the Portuguese is decent and (2) if you could give me the Portuguese version of the two quotations from the Bible at the bottom of the page, corresponding to the inscription on the door of the Chapel of Senhor das Barrocas in Aveiro. I should therefore return the same sheet with the annotations I am requesting.
>
> Regarding this chapel, do you know of any publication about it by Dr F. Ferreira Neves, which according to the Inventário de Aveiro (south zone), p. 146, contains the demarcation dates of the work? Father Nogueira Gonçalves does not cite the title of the publication, although he publishes the same dates, praising the author's industry. As you can see, I am working on the problem of the architecture of the Library of Coimbra, encouraged by a letter that came from the Vice-Rector, in which she showed great interest in the project of writing a critical monograph of the building"[19].

On 10th May 1971, he quickly writes to Flávio:

> "there is no longer any need to review the atrocious translations of Latin words in Coimbra Library, because, being in

[19] MLRP. *Flávio Gonçalves estate. Epistolography of Robert C. Smith*, letter of 24th April 1971.

> Washington last week, I found the book Coimbra Antiga e Moderna by António Cardoso Borges de Figueiredo, in which there are excellent Portuguese versions made by his father (...) but I always hope to be able to get the others from the Book of St. Matthew quoted in my letter"[20].

In the epistolographic collection of Flávio Gonçalves, there is a copy of a letter Smith wrote to Avelino Jesus da Costa. This was a common practice between them, as we have identified some letters written by Smith to other personalities, of which he sent a copy to Flávio. It is dated 10th July 1971:

> "Remembering the pleasure I had in our visit last January in Coimbra, I am sorry I will not be able to return during this summer to finish the research I am doing on the University Library building. The reason is that I have decided to devote this holiday period to revising the text of a book on European furniture to be published in London"[21].

This is the first indication that we know of, in which the North American historian admits that other work to which he had formally committed himself, in this case with the British publisher Phaidon to write a book on European furniture, could prevent him from immediately continuing his research into the King João Library. After the great investment made in the first half of the year, when he contacted several people to help him with his research, another situation began to emerge in July, which was reinforced in his letter to Professor Manuel Lopes de Almeida on 12th July. In this letter,

---

[20] *Idem.*

[21] *Idem.*

in the wake of what he had already done on the church stalls[22], he tells the academic, who is working on a book about Portuguese pulpits, that:

> "At present that research and also my work on the Library building are suspended until I finish a book on European furniture which I am preparing for the Phaidon Publishing House in London. As the task is a big one, with 800 prints, I had to devote the whole summer to it, and how many more months it will take I do not yet know. I was sorry, however, not to return to Coimbra, where in January I had the great pleasure of conversing with my illustrious Friend and Colleague, who helped me so much and so kindly"[23].

Smith did not return to Portugal in 1971 and in November of the same year, he told Flavio of his disillusionment with the country, personified in its institutions[24]. In this and other letters, he complains about the slowness, the bureaucracy, the lack of organisation and cooperation, in short, the obstacles to his work. The publications he had in press were not developing, especially the work in which he had invested most and which he considered his best: the book dedicated to Friar José de Santo António Ferreira Vilaça, the Benedictine sculptor. Various vicissitudes, including the delays and diversion of the proofs he sent to Portugal and which were sent back to the United States, and the long-time (over a year) he waited for Azeredo Perdigão's preface exasperated the historian and deprived him of the desire to return to work in Portugal. That winter everything haunted him.

---

[22] Smith, R. C. (1968) - *Cadeirais de Portugal*. Livros Horizonte.

[23] MLRP. *Flávio Gonçalves estate*. Epistolography of Robert C. Smith. Copy of Smith's letter to Professor Manuel Lopes de Almeida, 12th July 1971.

[24] *Idem*, 21st November 1971.

1972 saw new prospects for his work and there are several letters in which he refers to the multiple activities that plunged him into the conclusion of old projects and the avalanche of new ones he wanted to embrace. He tells Egídio Guimarães, on 9th May, that a first version of his "new Benedictine study, this time on Nossa Senhora da Estrela in Lisbon and the Cabanas convent is almost finished[25], then he states:

> "Regarding the two books about Braga, which are with Livros Horizonte, I'm rather discouraged. As for Friar José de Santo António I spent months, as you know, struggling with the index and the preface. Everything was ready by mid-winter, the [Livros Horizonte] promised publication before Easter. But nothing happened, nor did they answer my letters (...) I have been waiting since last summer for the second proofs of André Soares (...) Perhaps I would have more results if I went there myself, but with the fall of our currency I cannot even consider the idea of travelling"[26].

On 5th June, he wrote to him again. This time it was on matters related to the great congress in honour of André Soares, which was being prepared[27]; and on Porto City Hall's request to publish a book commemorating the 200th anniversary of Nicolau Nasoni's death, summarising the data from the one he had published in 1967[28]. He also mentioned that the issue of the *Apollo* Magazine dedicated to

---

[25] Cf. Smith, R.C. (1972). Dois Estudos Beneditinos. *Boletim da Academia Nacional de Belas-Artes*. 27 69-101.

[26] Letter from Smith to Egídio Guimarães. *Egídio Guimarães estate*.

[27] Congress in honour of André Soares, which took place in Braga and Porto between 6th and 11th April 1973 and in which Robert Smith participated with important functions, such as chairman, speaker and tour guide of the monuments of the two cities. See the publication: A arte em Portugal no século XVIII. (1973-1974). *Bracara Augusta*. XVII and XVIII.

[28] Smith, R. C. (1966) - *Nicolau Nasoni, Arquitecto do Porto*. Livros Horizonte.

18th century Portuguese art[29] was due to come out shortly before the congress, as its editor Dennis Sutton had assured him. In the following month, he wrote again to Egídio Guimarães, telling him that the original and photographs of his new study on the sacristy of Braga Cathedral had been sent and that he would take care of the writing of the short book on Nasoni. He also informed him that he was still working to have his book about Aleijadinho in Congonhas do Campo[30] published. A good occasion for its launching would be "in the great exhibition of Brazilian baroque art, in Washington, in November... so this is my latest news. I will not tell you about the "national" activities, which continue to increase. I have a very full life and I hope my health will continue to support it!"[31].

The book about Congonhas do Campo reached him in August 1972, as he tells Egídio in a letter dated the 14th of that month. Smith returned to Portugal, in October 1972, to finalize the preparations for the congress honouring André Soares.

In 1973, he resumed his research on the Joanina Library. In the midst of other letters to his correspondents abroad, we found one to Yves Bottineau (1925-2008)[32] dated 15th may 1973. Smith asked Bottineau for copies of rare engravings by Jean Berain from the National Library of Paris. He was interest in drawings of the back of a carriage. Yves Bottineau contacted the director of the National Library of Paris, who replied that he had nothing on the engraving Smith was looking for, which was entitled: "Deriere du

---

[29] *Apollo*. XCVII, 134, April 1973.

[30] Smith, R.C. (1973) - *Congonhas do Campo*. Agir.

[31] Letter from Smith to Egídio Guimaraes. *Egídio Guimarães estate*.

[32] French art historian, he was a specialist in Spanish and Portuguese art of the seventeenth and eighteenth centuries. He Taught art history at the Université Paris Ouest Nanterre La Défense. Was appointed curator in the department of objets d'art of the Louvre Museum, later became general inspector of museums. In 1986 he was appointed chief curator of the museum and national estate of Versailles and the Trianons.

Premier Carosse doré". He said that these prints were published by A. Guérinet and R.A. Weigert, dedicated to Jean Berain (1937) and were wrongly attributed. He refers to the library of the École Nationale des Beaux Arts as a possibility for research[33].

Scattered in the Robert C. Smith Archive are annotations on various 17th and 18th century ornament books, mostly by French ornamentists[34], such has *Ornatos- cahier de príncipes d´ornements dessinés par caillot et graves par Lucien*; *Premier livre de Trophées contenant divers atributtes d´église* by J.C. de la Fosse; *Expressions des Passions de L´ame representées en plusiers testes gravées aprés les dessins de feu de Monsieur le Brun* and *Les proportions du corps humain- mesurées sur les plus belles figures de l´antiquité* by Girard Audrass.

Through his notes and letters, we understand that the issue of foreign aesthetic and decorative influences in the Joanina library was one of the most relevant focuses of his study, although in his text, namely on the second chapter, this is not fully perceptible.

Returning to his correspondence with colleagues in Portugal, Maria Helena da Rocha Pereira, in a letter dated 25th January, replying to another letter by Smith states that:

> "I have the greatest pleasure in collaborating with you in the Braga Congress[35], where I hope we will have the opportunity to talk about many of the subjects that your magnificent studies have revealed and clarified.
>
> As soon as I received your letter, I transmitted the request to the Director of the General Library of the University, my esteemed colleague and friend, Prof G. Braga da Cruz.

[33] CGF. *The Robert C. Smith Archive*. Box. 8, folder "França".

[34] *Idem*. Box 47.

[35] The Braga Congress to which Maria Helena da Rocha Pereira refers is the one mentioned above, in homage to André Soares.

I am sending you the indications as he sent them, since they may be useful to you. Meanwhile, in accordance with your instructions, I have written directly to Mr. Anthony Sutton, providing him with the information about the measurements of the portrait of King João V"[36].

After the congress, in the spring, Smith travelled through Portugal, stopping at Aveiro, Coimbra, Torres Vedras, Sintra and Setúbal, "to do research and take photographs for future books"[37].

On that occasion he writes to Flávio Gonçalves, from the Hotel Flórida in Lisbon, where he used to stay in the city:

"Last Sunday, in Aveiro, I was lucky enough to find the Church of the Senhor das Barrocas open, and there I managed, with the *agrément* of a brother, to work alone for hours.

The following day:

"I worked all day in the King João Library, taking countless photographs. On Tuesday I met Doctor César Pegado, who put at my disposal several books that I wanted to consult, through which I formed a "plan de guerre" for the archive. There I was lucky, because in the book of revenues and expenses, I found an unprecedented world of information about the University's works during the reign of King João V. Suffice it to say that I know who painted the beautiful ceiling of the rectory chapel, how much it cost, etc. who added to the portrait of King João V in 1724, the primitive colours of the interior of the Library, and much more (...) From the archives of the Direção dos Monumentos Nacionais,

---

[36] CGF. *The Robert C. Smith Archive*. Box. 1.

[37] MLRP. *Flávio Gonçalves estate. Epistolography of Robert C. Smith.*

I obtained the dates of the renovation work on the exterior of the same building, as well as a precious old photograph of the primitive façade and a proof for Nuno Tasso de Sousa, who is to make a complete elevation of the flank"[38].

By mid-1973, Smith was deep into the issues raised by the Library building, this time by the alterations made to its exterior, dating from 1943. In a letter dated 2nd July 1973, written from his farm in Glenmore, Pennsylvania, to the architect Nuno Tasso de Sousa, he mentions that he had been to Coimbra and lucky "in his research into the interior of the Library, having found important news about the portrait of King João V, paintings of the rooms, etc. But the enigma of the pilasters or wedges outside remains"[39]. Due to the relevance of the content, longer extracts from this letter are transcribed:

> "Talking in Coimbra with the architects of the National Monuments, I found that those stone [pilasters] that are on the east (main) and south façade were introduced by the Public Works in 1943 and immediately following years. There was even a photograph from that time showing the walls, before the works, without pilasters in the upper area, which corresponds to the three grandiose reading rooms. The architect José Amoroso Lopes Júnior very kindly gave me a proof of this photograph and I was left to offer another to my friend.
>
> In this curious photograph, one sees, together with the four side bands and other details subsequently lost, the walls without pilasters and the windows without the stone frames given them in 1943, while the windows of the west and north facades have remained as shown in my photograph in reference to

38 *Idem*. 29th April 1973.

39 Nuno Tasso de Sousa's personal archive. *Letters by Robert C. Smith*.

> these, entirely without frames. There are two smooth concentric surfaces of a style reminiscent, as my friend has rightly said, of Sir John Soane and early 19th century classicism. I do not see any Portuguese building in the whole of the 18th century with openings without stone frames or angular pilasters, so that these must be of the 18th century, like the windows of the top floor of the D. Maria II National Theatre. Were they all modified at that time along with the walls themselves, in some attempt at modernisation? But where to find the respective documentation? I have searched, to no avail, all the publications about the Library of Coimbra, some of them very extensive. It is possible that there is some reference never mentioned in the books of revenue and expenditure. They exist and I shall consult them when I return in November, but it will take a long time, as I have no idea of the date of this possible modification".

It is thus clear that the Library building had been altered in its exterior appearance in the mid-20th century by suppressing architectural elements and, in some cases, replacing them with others. Robert C. Smith's perplexity about some of the compositional choices of the building's exterior is paraded in this letter, which is essential for a better understanding of the depth of his investigation of the building, the methods used in that process, and most importantly, the finding of significant interventions in the building's model.

The letter goes on to raise questions about these choices to alter the façade and elevations of the Library. Smith hypothesises that these changes made by the National Monument architects in 1943 may have been partly inspired by the 1772 Pombaline plan, which provided for an extension to the Library.

> "In the Library archives, there is a plan that I photographed. I then sent the negative to Casa Alvão in Porto, asking for an

enlargement to be sent to you. This plan is curious and very useful. It dates from 1772 when the Marquis of Pombal, being in Coimbra, decided to destroy the current University chapel to make another one parallel to the King João Library, which would be reproduced on the other side (north) of the new chapel, thus giving more space for books. According to this plan and an accompanying drawing, the entrance to the two libraries would be through the chapel doorway. Well, the 1772 plan, never, of course, executed, is useful to us for several reasons. Firstly, it seems to indicate the presence of pilasters on the façades, which more or less correspond to those erected in 1943. Secondly, it shows the position of the six grand tables distributed between the three reading rooms. Would it not, therefore, be possible to use this plan of 1772 for the plan you are going to make for my book, remembering, of course, the fact that the gateway is missing, having been suppressed by the Marquis' architect, in obedience to the new Pombaline triple formula?

As for the side elevation of the Library, which you stayed to prepare as well, I think there should be no problem with the three lower floors. In the last one, the pilasters below should be continued, keeping the beautiful stone bands, the complete triglyphs and the "shelves" with their punches visible in the photograph taken before the 1943 works. The six small rectangular windows with their simple stone frames would be removed, perhaps another proof that the large gaps above were also edged with stone in their primitive form".

This long letter was a stage for discussion about the alterations made to the exterior of the Library and how the plan of the building could be drawn up today. However, we also see that Robert C. Smith wanted Tasso de Sousa to draw up a plan of the building and make drawings of its elevations. These were to be as close as possible to what he suspected was the original, before the 1943 intervention, still visible in the photographs he mentions from before the National Monuments works. He ends the letter to 'his' architect by saying:

> "I hope that when you have the time and inclination, you will let me know your ideas about these complicated problems. I am excited about this book, after having talked to the publisher in Lisbon [Carlos Moura of Livros Horizonte] and the director of the Library in Coimbra, but everything depends on the plan and design that only you can execute."

On the 18th July, Guilherme Braga da Cruz wrote to Smith from Coimbra in these terms:

> "My dear colleague and friend Prof Robert C. Smith
> (...) We are all looking forward to your planned book on the Joanina Library. God grant you courage, life and health to bring this and other works to a good end (...).
> Accept an affectionate hug from your colleague, admirer and very grateful friend"[40].

Smith's research on Coimbra's great library was echoed by the university leaders, namely the director of the General Library (1971-1977), the aforementioned Professor Guilherme Braga da Cruz; the Vice-Rector, Professor Maria Helena da Rocha Pereira; Canon Avelino Jesus da Costa and Manuel Lopes de Almeida, among other Coimbra intellectuals and academics.

On 30th August 1973, Smith wrote again to Egídio Guimarães, reporting on the completion of his book on Nicolau Nasoni[41];

---

40 CGF. *The Robert C. Smith Archive*. Box. 1, doc. 18b.

41 The summary book commissioned by Porto City Hall to celebrate the 200th anniversary of Nasoni's death.

the article on the role of painter Manuel da Silva in the Coimbra library[42], which was sent to and received by those who directed the literary supplement of the journal *Comércio do Porto*; as well as the biography of Quervelle, the architect[43].

He thought of coming to Portugal in November to work on a new project as a grant recipient from the Calouste Gulbenkian Foundation. His intention was to publish a monograph, which he later entitled "Miscellany of Art Studies and Social History of the 18th and 19th centuries in Portugal". "In the meantime, however," he wrote to Egídio Guimarães, "I have to finish the book by Agostinho Marques". A new letter sent in October says that he would have to postpone his coming to Portugal, as he was immersed in the book, *Agostinho Marques*, "which turned out much larger than I had thought. The truth is that I decided to enter the question of the trade of assembler in Portugal and Brazil"[44].

He returned to Portugal in early 1974 and in that year his favourite interlocutor was Egídio Guimarães. He wrote several letters to him, both in Portugal and the United States: "I find myself in a truly painful situation, because it seems I will have to abandon all my work here, perhaps permanently (...) I am seriously ill with a strange disease, which seems to be gouty rheumatism". On 3rd March, he bade farewell to his friend saying that he was leaving for the USA due to a heart complication, but soon afterwards, on the 11th of the same month, in an enthusiastic letter, stated that he was better and working on the material he had collected: "the many notes and photographs made during the last two months". He

---

42 Smith, R. C. (1973). O pintor Manuel da Silva na Universidade de Coimbra. *O Comércio do Porto*. 291, 23rd October.

43 Series of 5 articles on the furniture of Anthony Quervelle, entitled: The furniture of Anthony G. Quervelle, published in *Antiques*, Part I: May 1973, vol. 103, n°5; part II: July 1973, vol. 104, n°1; part III: August 1973, vol. 104, n°2; part IV: January 1974, vol. 105, n°1; part V: March 1974, vol. 105, n°3.

44 Letter of 29th October. *Egídio Guimarães estate*.

emphasises the work on *Agostinho Marques*, the search for a new publisher and the new information he has gathered[45]:

> "large consignment of photographs taken by me during my last visit, which guarantee the publication, in Bracara Augusta of several studies of mine, including one about the tiles of Casa dos Biscainhos. I also have all the photographic documentation for the article for Fine Arts, about the Tibães railings and their Benedictine offspring (...) I soon started working on problems of our art, so that I already have an article written and approved by the director of a New York magazine."

This was also the year when he reaffirmed that the academics in Coimbra continued to support his work and to remind him of their unconditional support and the relevance that they attributed to the research that he carried out. The work on the King João Library was much desired in Coimbra:

> "I was also very pleased to learn that one of the works that you intend to continue, in this phase of relative rest, is the one about our Library. I do not need to tell you that whatever you may need here in Coimbra and in this house of yours, which is the General Library of the University, it will be our pleasure to serve you"[46].

Nevertheless, Smith had a commitment on his hands that he could no longer postpone due to contractual obligation: the writing of the book dedicated to European furniture that the London publisher, Phaidon, had commissioned him to write. In addition to

---

[45] Letter of 8th April 1974. *Egídio Guimarães estate.*

[46] Letter of 24th March 1974. *The Robert C. Smith Archive.* Box. 1.

his writing commitments, his life in the United States was still full of tasks and requests. Retired on disability from the University of Pennsylvania, where he taught until 1972, the prospect of greater freedom to continue his studies of Portuguese Baroque art sometimes inspired him to the point of euphoria. At other times, we find a Robert C. Smith demoralized and frustrated with Portugal, a country which, according to him, stubbornly failed to respond to his requests, whether they were for the publication of his works or the streamlining of bureaucratic mechanisms, which delayed the response to the realisation of projects and ideas that he presented to the different departments of culture and heritage, publishers and private entities.

Among the many health problems mentioned in letters exchanged with some of his best friends in Portugal were cardiac issues, gout and the great motor difficulties he sometimes felt when he undertook tiring journeys. He especially complained about his stay in Coimbra, where he was dedicated to the study of the Joanina in early 1974. The orography of the city was not beneficial to him, with so many ups and downs, as he confesses to Egídio Guimarães in March 1974, even mentioning that he was forced to suspend his work for months[47] .

It is, however, a lively Robert C. Smith and keen to complete the book on the Library that comes across in a letter to Nuno Tasso de Sousa, written from his farm in Glenmore, Pennsylvania, on 27th May 1974:

> "I was delighted with the plan of the Joanina Library of Coimbra, many aspects of whose history still remain dark despite all my efforts made in situ. I have therefore decided to do the book without

[47] Letter to Egídio Guimarães on 3rd March 1974. CGF. *The Robert C. Smith Archive*. Box. 1.

> being able to offer all the desirable explanations. I intend to devote the summer to this task, which I hope to see largely finished when, if all goes well, I return to Portugal in October"[48] .

It was only in August 1974, through a letter addressed to Egídio Guimarães, that the progress of the book he dedicated to the Joanina library could be glimpsed for the first time. In it, Smith says he is entirely dedicated to the new book, which has been occupying him for years, and that it was through this book project that he contacted several Coimbra archivists, with the best results. The chapter on the history of construction was ready, in which the figure of the master builder Gaspar Ferreira appears for the first time, in his words, "l'homme à tout faire de l'Université". He reveals that he will pay more attention to the figure who, in his opinion, was responsible for designing most of the building, Claude de Laprade. To this end, Smith asks for help in accessing a proof of Ayres de Carvalho's communication on Claude de Laprade at the conference honouring André Soares, as the publication was in press, indicating that he will write to Francisco Pereira de Bacelar Ferreira[49] on the same subject[50] .

He continued writing to Egídio Guimarães during the last months of 1974. In September, he confessed that he had to abandon the planned trip to Portugal due to work commitments with the Phaidon Publishing House in London, stating that the book had been commissioned in 1969 and that the publishers were pressuring him. "It's going to take months and months but perhaps in the spring I'll be able to get rid of this big responsibility[51]. On Christmas Eve, he wrote again to his friend:

---

[48] Nuno Tasso de Sousa's personal archive. *Letters by Robert C. Smith.*

[49] One of the editors of the journal *Bracara Augusta.*

[50] Letter of 19th August 1974. *Egídio Guimarães estate.*

[51] Letter of 1st September 1974. *Idem.*

"I feel a great desire to renew my Portuguese studies, suspended for months because of the other project that has taken me so long.

I want to fetch some *azulejos* I need in Évora and Estremoz, analyse those of the Casa Anadia in Mangualde, review monuments of northern woodcarving attributable to my great Gabriel Rodrigues Álvares, and finally, if I may, receive, in Braga, the coveted City Medal, awarded almost two years ago"[52] .

Smith had another passion on the horizon: the deeper study of Baroque tiles[53]. With the disappearance of the great Portuguese tile scholar, João Miguel dos Santos Simões (1907-1972), Smith felt more at ease to enter this world that had always fascinated him and that he intrinsically linked to his studies of the art of Portuguese carving. In his timid forays into the field, he always referred to the studies of Santos Simões, recognising in that historian the excellence of his method of study and his profound knowledge of the subject. It was natural that in the lifetime of Santos Simões, Smith had been somewhat reverent and shy of venturing into the master's territory.

Smith visited Portugal again between February and March 1975. He stopped at Braga, Viseu, Mangualde, Coimbra and Évora; writing letters to Egídio Guimarães, from Lisbon, Coimbra and Évora. In one of these letters, he told Guimarães: "I am here for a short time and the main purpose of this visit is to work in Coimbra, where I will be staying at Hotel Bragança from 3rd March." In the last year of his life, he did intense research in Coimbra and that is what he

[52] Letter of 23rd December 1974. *Idem*.

[53] The subject of the tiling had always been cherished in his studies, see for instance: "Smith, R.C. (1966). A new museum of tiles in Lisbon. *Antiques*. 98,6, 828-833; *Idem*. (1968). Azulejos of Cascais. *The Journal of the American Portuguese Cultural Society*. II, 4, 1-15; *Idem*. (1968). Ceramics: The Tiles. *The Art of Portugal: 1500-1800* (pp. 229-236). Weidenfeld and Nicolson; *Idem*. (1970). Três Estudos Bracarenses. *Belas Artes*. 2.ª série, 24-26, 49-83; *Idem*. (1973). French Models for Portuguese Tiles. *Apollo*. 97, 134, 396-407; *Idem*. (1975). Some Lisbon Tiles in Estremoz. *The Journal of the American Portuguese Cultural Society*. IX, 2, 1-17.

continued to talk about to his friend from Braga. He told Guimarães he took great pleasure in his visit to Braga, the day before making "a series of discoveries in the Coimbra University archives[54]", which would greatly enrich the two books he was working on. He mentioned stays in Viseu and Mangualde and the trip to Estremoz to photograph tiles. He embarked for the United States to spend Easter at home on 29th March, planning another visit to Portugal in November.

In April, he wrote to Egídio Guimarães again, regretting that the series of conferences he was holding in Atlanta (according to the enclosed brochure) did not allow him to continue with his new work, only possible due to the great success of his research in Coimbra.

Among the "wonderful things" found, under the tutelage of Dr Lígia, is "the date of death of Manuel da Silva, the painter of the shelves at the Royal Library; all the dates of Gaspar Ferreira; immense information about the tiles in Coimbra, its painters and tents; and many other things". The success of the photographic campaign gave him a lot of material to publish, and he added that, after leaving Coimbra, his work on tiles continued to be successful[55].

From April 1975, the archivist of the University of Coimbra Library, Lígia Brandão, began a series of shipments of photocopied documents and plans. On 18th April, she wrote informing him that she had found the receipt signed by Friar Cipriano da Cruz, who made the image of St Catherine, existing in the University of Coimbra chapel. She also sent a photocopy, actually attached to the letter, as well as its transcription[56]. In this letter, she further added other documents referring to works by artists who were contracted for

---

[54] Letter of 26th March 1975. *Egídio Guimarães estate.*

[55] *Idem.*

[56] 18th April 1975, letter to Egídio Guimarães. CGF. *The Robert C. Smith Archive.* Cx. 1, doc. 14a.

work at the university and its patronage in the 17th and 18th centuries. Goldsmiths, carvers, sculptors, painters, potters, carpenters, tinsmiths, gilders, parade in brief transcriptions of works.

The last two known letters that the aforementioned archivist sent to Smith date from July 1975: one on the 23rd and the other on the 31st[57]. In both, information regarding Smith's requests is exchanged, along with photocopies of various documents, either referring to the architect Macamboa, including a watercolour plan for one of the churches in the university's patronage, or more documents referring to the Joanina Library. The archivist tells him that she is convinced that in November he will make great discoveries in the university archive. The last missive, dated 31st July 1975, highlights Smith's excellent idea regarding the study of the Coimbra environment, as he did in the book dedicated to Fr. José de Santo António Vilaça, in Braga. In the penultimate month of his life, July 1975, he was still enthusiastic about the Joanina book project, as can be read in a letter to Flávio Gonçalves:

> "I was very lucky. Invited by Yale University to deliver a speech on a national matter, I had the opportunity to locate, in one of the libraries there, the precious engravings by Salomon Kleiner of the university, I mean the Imperial Library of Vienna, which date from 1735[58]. I saw at once that there was a definite relationship to Paulus Decker's much earlier engravings of Nuremberg for palaces of princes, which was never indicated. With photographs of these two series of engravings, it will be possible to establish the great originality of the Portuguese library and, at the same time, the features that it has in common with the engravings. I am now

[57] *Idem*.

[58] Visualization of various prints by Salomon Kleiner in https://www.gettyimages.com.br/fotos/salomon-kleiner.

slowly incorporating, in my chapter on the history of the building, the many important new items that I gathered during the happy weeks that I spent in March in the university city"[59].

On 18th August 1975, three days before his death, he wrote a premonitory letter to his friend Flávio Gonçalves:

> "Speaking of clichés (in the photographic sense), I am delighted to put at your disposal all the ones I have in any branch of Portuguese artistic expression. But send your list now, now, so that when you arrive, you'll find me still alive. It's the anniversary of my father's death at the same age I am now (and also the same illness that killed him) (...) I've just written an article about the tiles of Estremoz for a magazine here (...) I have almost completed the entirely redone chapter on the history of the Joanina Library in Coimbra, the first of my book dedicated to this monument. It has taken a long time and will still take a lot of time but I think it is worth it. For you, D. Lígia and Jorge Peixoto I intend to send copies, hoping that they will inspire criticism from you. With a big hug
>
> Roberto".

Final note

The unpublished work by Robert C. Smith dedicated to the history and art of the Joanina Library of Coimbra is the first major systematization of the constructive history of this monument, which

---

59 BRP. *Flávio Gonçalves estate. Epistolography by Robert C. Smith.* Letter to Flávio, July 23rd 1975. About the prints by Paulo Decker that he refers to, see https://gallica.bnf.fr/ark:/12148/btv1b10501722r/f80.item.zoom.

also presents scientifically sustained progress on the proposal of authorship for the design of its façade and interiors.

It is an integrated look at the work, highlighting, albeit not exhaustively, the role of the Manuel de Moura Manuel, rector of the university from 1685-1690, Bishop of Bragança-Miranda from 1690 to 1699 and commissioner of the tombs and the altar of the Chapel of Nossa Senhora da Penha de França at Quinta da Vista Alegre, in Ílhavo from the sculptor Claude Laprade. It similarly underscores the roles of Nuno da Silva Teles (uncle), rector between 1694 and 1702, commissioner of the Portico and the overdoors of the *Gerais* classes from the same sculptor and his homonymous nephew, rector from 1715 to 1718, who gave impetus to the construction process of the new Library. The directorates of Pedro Sanches de Baena (1719-1722) and Francisco Carneiro de Figueiroa (1722-1745) were also decisive, as they closely followed the work on the Library[60].

The vital role played by the university rectors in the works, with certainly a say in the chosen artists, whether for the reform of the *Gerais*, or later in the construction of the Joanina Library, is also understood by their position as members of influential families, close to the Royal House. If we study their various family trees, their training in the privileged colleges of Coimbra, namely those of São Pedro and São Paulo and the influence they had, not only directly on the university, but also on its patronage, we can clearly see that they would be able to suggest architects, designers, sculptors and other artists for work on the Library[61]. This is probably what

60 Cf. *Reitores dos séculos XVII a XIX*. https://www.uc.pt/sobrenos/historia/reitores_xvii_xix.

61 See Fonseca, F. T. (2007). The Social and Cultural Roles of the University of Coimbra (1537-1820). Some Considerations", *e-Journal of Portuguese History*, 5 1-21. https://www.brown.edu/Departments/Portuguese_Brazilian_Studies/ejph/html/issue9/html/ffonseca_main.html.

happened with the sculptor Claude de Laprade, an old acquaintance of the rectors Manuel de Moura Manuel, Nuno da Silva Telles and his namesake nephew.

Robert C. Smith's analysis innovates by treating the Library's work with the most uncompromising look of a foreigner, without nationalist atavisms, despite his well-known appreciation of Portuguese baroque art. His work was interpretative, comparing the Joanina Library with other contemporary works in Portugal and abroad, mainly in France and Italy. He listed artists and stylistically appreciated their work. This method led to the works of the sculptor and designer Claude Laprade, in line with what had already been advanced by the researcher Ayres de Carvalho[62], but with the addition of a meticulous stylistic reading of the work. This journey made it possible to compare and search for Laprade's own styles, confronting the Library's decorative work with other documented works by that same artist.

The research for the book dedicated to the Great Library of Coimbra had other consequences beyond that objective. Robert C. Smith collected dozens of documents about art and artists present in monuments of the university's patronage, which include, among others, contracts for carving, gilding and other crafts, which he completed by consulting parish records of baptisms, marriages and deaths.

With all these rich sources at his disposal, which he had been accumulating since the end of the sixties, Smith also intended to

---

Figueirôa-Rêgo, J. (2013). Das instâncias académicas de Coimbra ao Santo Ofício e à Mesa da Consciência e Ordens: in(ter)dependencia(s), sociabilidades e interesses. (pp. 249-271). In Fátima F., Hermínia V. V. e Mafalda S.C (eds.). *Centros Periféricos de Poder na Europa do Sul (Séculos XII-XVIII)*. Colibri-CIDEHUS/EU e López-Salazar, A.I. (2017). Una oligarquía eclesiástica en Portugal durante el antiguo régimen: catedráticos, canónigos e inquisidores. *Librosdelacorte.es MONOGRÁFICO*. 6, 9, 164-184.

[62] Carvalho, A. (1957). Desvenda-se o caso do misterioso artista Claude Laprade. *Diário de Lisboa*. 37, 7 April.

write a monograph in which he would present the biographies and study other artists in the Coimbra region and their works. Testimony to this are the notes he left in his professional estate. Through the great research he carried out on the Library, Smith collected more material than he was able to systematize and publish. For the same reason, this research proved to be a larger project with the crossing of much information, whether documental, visual or cartographic. This data derived from the countless conversations he had with academics from Coimbra and other regions; with those interested in heritage and authors of local history; with archivists and librarians. All these meetings were fundamental to articulate an enormous source of information that he collected personally or that came to him through the kindness of his multiple and well-placed interlocutors.

For Robert C. Smith, the artistic and symbolic ballast of the Joanina Library did not end in the strict circle of contemporary monuments in the city of Coimbra, such as the sacristy of the Church of Santo António dos Olivais. It went further and left its mark on buildings such as the Church of Senhor das Barrocas, in Aveiro or on other buildings not yet studied in the patronage of the University, which have works by some artists who worked on the Joanina Library.

The Library's echoes go far beyond the contemporary influences it may have had. Among many others that will certainly exist are the Quinta Patiño Library, in Estoril; the Chinese Room of the Faculty of Law of the University of Coimbra and the portrait of Luís I in the senate room of the Portuguese Parliament[63], similar to that of João V at the Royal Library of Coimbra.

---

[63] Cf. Antes e Depois | Sala do Senado (1867-2017) (2017). *Boletim da Assembleia da República- Comunicar*, https://app.parlamento.pt/comunicar/Artigo.aspx?ID=879. The room, designed in 1856 by the architect Jean-François Colson (active in Portugal between 1855 and 1863) and later adapted by António Tomás da Fonseca (c. 1822-1894), features a portrait of King Luís I by José Rodrigues (1828-1887). The carved

In recent years, monographs and articles have been published in scientific journals addressing some concrete aspects of the rich history and art of the Library. Nevertheless, this work now being published, after almost 50 years, remains important. This is not only due to the information it conveys but, above all, because of the areas it opens up for future research into the rich artistic heritage of the Library and other baroque monuments in the Coimbra region, and the patronage of its university.

frame and its sculptural components are by the carver, Leandro Braga (1839-1897), cf. also Mourão, C. (2009). Sala do Senado. História e Iconografia. (pp.17-37). In Teresa P. (ed.). *Sala do Senado*. Assembleia da República-divisão de edições.

Fig. 1 Portrait of D. Luís. Room of the senate of the Assembleia da República. Portugal. Gabinete de Estudos Olisiponenses

Fig. 2. Library of the Quinta Patiño. Estoril. Portugal
© António Moutinho/Portugal Sotheby's International Reality

Fig. 3. "Chinese room". Faculty of Law. University of Coimbra. Portugal

PRESENTATION

Coimbra University library is one of the oldest Portuguese buildings that most surprises and delights visitors. Financed by King João V (1706-1750), in 1717-1718, the Royal Protector of the University (1), this has been so since it was built, with this regal edifice escaping the general discredit that, for many years, the national baroque style underwent. The 'Library House'[64], as 18th century documents call it, has been subject to fulsome compliments both from foreigners and the Portuguese since its inauguration. Francisco Carneiro de Figueiroa, the dean who completed it, proclaimed the Coimbra library "one of the most magnificent in this Kingdom"[65]. (2) For Count Atanazy Raczynski, the scholarly Polish diplomat who produced the first History of Art in Portugal, the library was "la plus belle, la plus richement ornée, que j´aie jamais visiteé"[66]. (3)

In 1887, when the baroque style started to suffer from an almost universal contempt that only faded out after World War II, the Viscount of Villa-Maior lauded the "elegant and most beautiful Library".[67] Two decades later, Albrecht Haupt, the second great na-

[64] In the original: "Caza da Livraria". Translator´s note.

[65] In the original: "huma das mais magnificas obras que tem este Reino". Translator´s note.

[66] "[T]he most beautiful, the most richly decorated that I have ever visited". Translator´s note.

[67] In the original: "elegante e belissima Biblioteca". Translator´s note. Visconde de Villa Maior. (1877) - *Exposição Succinta da Organisação actual da Universidade de Coimbra*. (p. 475.) Imprensa da Universidade.

tional art historian, found it a worthy partner to the Hofbibliothek in Vienna, Austria, one of the most famous 18th century monuments in Europe.[68] In 1960, Germain Bazin dedicated an article to the library, where he called it the queen of the university libraries.[69] More recently, the expert Anthony Hobson, concluded that it was, next only to the Austrian Hofbibliotek, the most beautiful 18th century purpose built library. Its design was, for Hobson, one of the major innovations in the history of libraries.[70]

Gathering such compliments over the centuries, the library has won its place amongst the architectural masterpieces of Europe. It has done so, however, without anyone knowing the name of the 'Library House' architect. The few 18th century writers that addressed the university never stated it, and nor do the rare surviving documents on the library's construction. There is not even an oral tradition about who designed the building. It grew like a large exotic flower in Coimbra, without local antecedents and without creating those stories surrounding its construction and the personalities connected to it that abound with most of the great buildings of Europe's past.

With the interest in 18th century works of art generated by the publication of the first volumes of the National Library of Lisbon's *Guia de Portugal* in the 1920s, the problem of the library architect's identity began to attract the attention of certain scholars. As it was a royal commission, and there was no local candidate, it was natural to seek him in Lisbon, amongst the architects and artists of the sovereign's court. In his capacity as "Protector of the

---

[68] Haupt, A. (s.d.) - *A arquitetura da renascença em Portugal.* (p. 247). J. Rodrigues Livreiros Editores.

[69] Bazin, G. (1960). La Bibliothèque la plus fausteuse que j´aie jamais vu. *Connaissance des Arts*, 100, 60-71.

[70] This must be from Hobson (1970) - *Great Libraries.* Weidenfeld & Nicolson. (pp. 85, 242-234 and 242, which is mentioned in the manuscript notes of Robert C. Smith. Hobson here refers to the *Biblioteca Joanina de Coimbra*.

Fig. 1 Aerial view of Paço das Escolas, with the Joanine library to the left of the image. Coimbra. Portugal © Nuno Antunes

Fig. 2 Portal of the Joanine Library. Coimbra. Portugal © Nuno Antunes

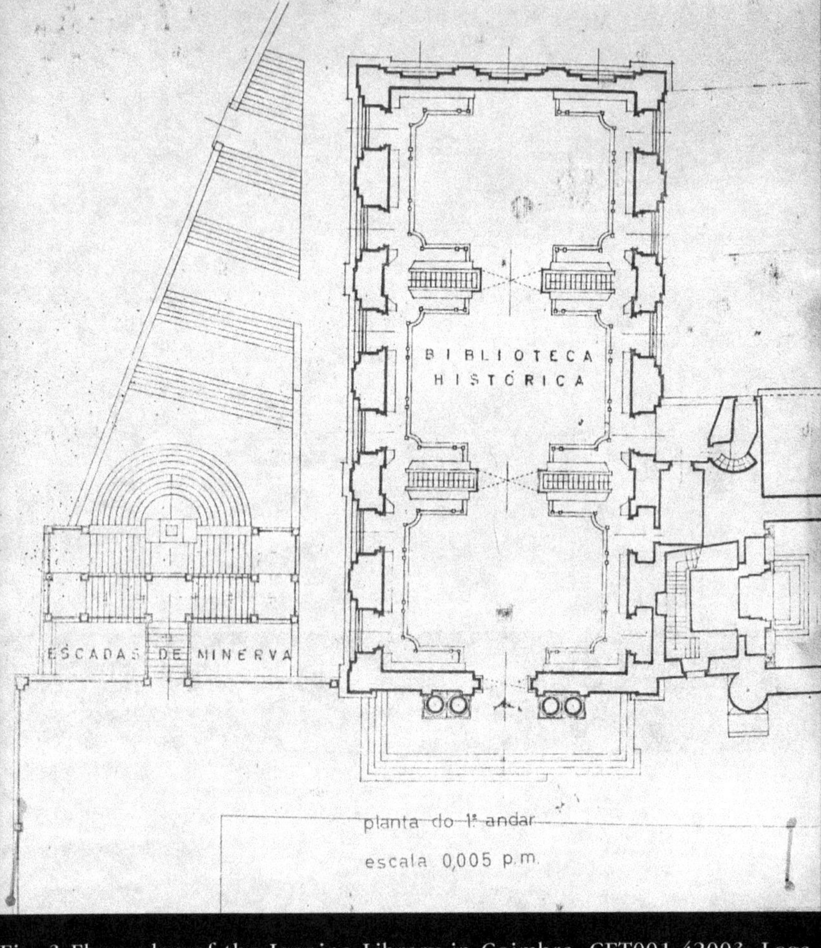

Fig. 3 Floor plan of the Joanina Library in Coimbra. CFT001.42003. Legado Robert Chester Smith, Fundação Calouste Gulbenkian, Biblioteca de Arte e Arquivos, Lisboa.

Fig. 4 Photo of Charles Thompson 1866. AUC (cota R-69-16 A)

University", the monarch would pay the considerable expenses that the enterprise incurred.

The leading figure among these was the German, Johann Friedrich Ludwig (1670-1752), called Lodovivi in Rome, where he learnt the art of goldsmithery. He then became Ludovice in Lisbon, where he arrived in 1701, called to Santo Antão by the Jesuits and where he began his fabulous career as an architect, with the plans for the royal palace, convent and basilica of Mafra, begun by order of João V in 1717.[71]

Ludovice spent the rest of his life in the service of the king, who appointed him chief architect of the kingdom of Portugal, in 1750,[72] and would spread throughout the Lisbon area a style almost literally based on the 17th century architecture and ornamental sculpture he had seen in Rome.

The first researcher to propose the name of João Frederico Ludovice as the Coimbra library architect was Xavier da Costa who, in 1932, attributed not only this building but also the university tower in 1728-1733 to him.[73] Regarding the library, da Costa's theory was generally supported by Reynaldo dos Santos, the greatest art authority in Portugal until his death in 1966.

Quite different, however, was the opinion of Vergílio Correia, the revered master of the history of art of Coimbra and surroundings, who, in his book, *Coimbra e arredores* stated that "the Library

---

71 Cf. Smith, R.C. (1936). Frederico Ludovice an eighteenth-century architect in Portugal. *The Art Bulletin*. 18 3, 273-370. More recently, Pimentel A.F. (2002). wrote about Mafra's architectural design, in *Arquitectura e Poder. O Real edifício de Mafra*. Livros Horizonte, and in (2017). Do convento de Mafra ao real edifício. *Monumentos*. 35, 38-51.

72 Questioned in the original. Robert C. Smith had already written Ludovice's biography, in which he indicated the exact date of recognition of the architect's services by King José I, during the reign of his father, João V, naming him chief architect of the kingdom. Cf. Smith, R.C. (1936). Frederico Ludovice an eighteenth-century architect in Portugal (...), 273-370.

73 Costa L. X. (1934) - *As belas-artes plásticas em Portugal durante o século XVIII*. (p.26). J. Rodrigues & Co.ª.

could not belong to the Master of Mafra, whose elegant and dry Italianism was incompatible with the massive Baroque-inspired 'Library House', both internally and externally a very Portuguese creation".[74] I broadly agree with this opinion, since the influences discernible in the library are, as we shall see, almost all Northern European rather than Italian.

For me, however, the library is far from being an entirely Portuguese work, as I shall show in due course.

As for the true 'Library House' architect, Professor Vergílio Correia never wanted to venture a more precise hypothesis, limiting himself, along with his collaborator in the *Inventário Artístico de Portugal*, to observing that "there is nevertheless a stylistic connection with other national works".[75]

Germain Bazin put forward another point of view. His curious suggestion was that the design for the Coimbra library had been sent from Vienna, whose imperial library, on Hofburg, was designed by Johann Fisher von Erlach the Elder in 1722, when the Coimbra library had already been partly completed. Inspired by the nationality of the then queen of Portugal, Mariana of Habsburg, sister of the emperor, together with a certain similarity between the Hofbibliothek and that of Coimbra, this hypothesis by Bazin supposes that "Jean V peut avoir en connaisance des intentions de son beau-frère d´elever une bibliothèque somptuese, intentions anteriores de plusiers anneés à l´exécution".[76]

---

[74] This short book was the result of a summer course organised by the Coimbra Faculty of Arts, and its authors, besides Vergílio Correia, included A. de Amorim Girão and Torquato de Souza Fernandes. Moreover, although this is not specified in the publication, it is legitimate to attribute, as Robert C. Smith did, the chapter dedicated to the University of Coimbra to Vergílio Correia. Cf. Girão, A. A., Correia, V., Fernandes, T. S. (1939) - *Coimbra e Arredores* (p. 85). Comissão Municipal de Turismo.

[75] Correia V., Gonçalves, A. N. (1947) - *Inventário Artístico de Portugal. Cidade de Coimbra* (p. 106). Academia Nacional de Belas Artes.

[76] Bazin, G. (1960). La Bibliothèque la plus fausteuse que j´aie jamais vu (...), 70. In French in the original.

Fig. 5 Interior of the Joanine Library. © Nuno Antunes

Fig. 6. National Library of Viena (Prunksaal). Austria.
©Art Kowalsky / Alamy Foto de stock

In fact, nothing justifies this assumption. It would actually be more reasonable to deduce the opposite: that the idea of the Hofburg and the other libraries, with their sumptuous rooms distinguishing 18th century Austria and Bavaria, came from Coimbra. Because all these libraries are later than the Portuguese one.

There remains a third theory that, for me, offers the only acceptable solution to the enigma. This is Claudio de Laprada's, based on the following. The main façade of the Coimbra library is distinctly French, depicted in etchings by Jean Le Pautre and Daniel Marot, two great Louis XIV ornamentalists and decorators. The pseudo-Chinese paintings inside the library reflect an exotic taste that, born in Paris and London in the second half of the 17th century, conquered the whole of Northern Europe in the first quarter of the following century.[77] And finally, the woodcarving inside the library, a marvellous adjunct to its Chinese features, is entirely Portuguese. It is fundamentally linked to the large gilded wooden altarpieces of the Joanine era, which began to appear in Lisbon in the 1710s and soon afterwards appeared in Porto and Coimbra.

In the light of these characteristics, one name inevitably emerges as a possible architect, at least for part of the Coimbra library.

---

[77] Research on Portuguese produced *Chinoiserie* used since the mid-17th century currently highlights the taste for this decorative option as a direct result of economic and artistic relations, mainly with China and Japan. See Gschwend, A. (2015). Olisipo, *Emporium Nobilissimum*: global consumption in renaissance Lisbon (p. 140-161). In AnneMarie G. and K.J.P. L. (eds.). *The global city on the streets of the renaissance*. Paul Holberton Publishing; Pimentel, A.F. (2013). Do Portugal exótico ao exotismo: o fenómeno da Chinoiserie em Portugal (96-109). In Alexandra C. (ed.). *O exótico nunca está em casa? A China na faiança e no azulejo portugueses (séculos XVII-XVIII)*. DGPC; Ferreira S. (2015). Reflexos em vermelho e ouro. Chinoiserie e talha ou a construção de um modelo de renovação artística (pp. 119-132). In Luís F. B. and Vítor S. (eds.). *Património Cultural Chinês em Portugal*. Centro Científico e Cultural de Macau. Ferreira S., Rosada M. (2023). A policromia poliédrica. Do douramento à *chinoiserie* no barroco luso-brasileiro. In Manuel G. L. y Francisco J. H. G. (eds.). *Color y Ornamento. Estudios sobre policromía en el mundo ibérico (s. XVII y XVIII)*. Universidad de Granada.

Smith, R.C. (1963) - *A Talha em Portugal*. (p. 117). Livros Horizonte.

As I pointed out in my book on Portuguese carving, *A Talha em Portugal* (1963), it is Claude de Laprada (Claude de Laprade). Born in Avignon in 1682[78], Laprada came to work in Portugal at a very young age. He first worked on the "Vista Alegre" estate chapel in Ílhavo (Aveiro) in 1699, where he masterfully executed two allegorical tombs in limestone, perhaps inaugurating there his career in woodcarving, and soon after at Coimbra University. Whilst there, from 1700 to 1702, he enhanced the entrance, courtyard and *Aulas dos Gerais* (School of General Studies) with a portico and a series of panels and allegorical images. This was done using the same regional limestone, strongly suggestive of contemporary religious and ornamental sculpture from Provence. Laprade later worked in Lisbon, where, until his death in 1738, he maintained one of the foremost woodcarving and stone sculpture workshops of the Joanine Baroque movement. With the undeniable success of his earlier works for Coimbra University, it was logical that he should be involved in the building of the library, whose basic plans were perhaps prepared in the royal *Aula de Arquitectura* (School of Architecture) in Lisbon, under the direction of Father Francisco Tinoco da Silva, "architect and master of the royal works and palaces of this city".[79] Thus, in 1964, the great scholar of Portuguese art of that period, Ayres de Carvalho, proposed that "we have not the slightest hesitation in stating that [Laprada] collaborated with Father Tinoco or even Ludwig in the sculptural decoration

[78] This birth date has been questioned by Ferreira S. (2017) - From stone to wood: Claude Laprade (c. 1675-1738) and his journey from Provence to Portugal (pp. 53-54). In Kathryn W., Jessica D., Matej K. (eds). *Artists and migration 1400-1850, Britain, Europe and beyond*. Cambridge Scholars Publishing.

[79] In the original: "architeto e mestre das obras e paços reaes desta cidade". Translator´s note. Concerning the life and work of the architect, Father Francisco Tinoco da Silva, see Coelho, T. C. (2014). *Os Nunes Tinoco, uma dinastia de arquitectos régios dos séculos XVII e XVIII*. (pp. 97-109). (Doctoral thesis in History of Art, Faculdade de Ciências Sociais e Humanas da Universidade Nova de Lisboa). I.

(drawings and models interpreted by local woodcarvers) at the University Library of Coimbra".[80]

Accepting the hypothesis of Claudio de Laprada's participation, with or without the *Aula de Arquitectura's* collaboration, immediately explains the abundance of sculpture both inside and outside the library. The stone pieces are intimately connected with his earlier works in Ílhavo and at the university; and the wooden images are equally suggestive of the Lisbon carvings that are only now beginning to be identified with the last phases of Claudio de Laprada's career. This also explains the character of the paintings in the library; the ceilings designed in a Lusitanian version of the Italian Baroque style triumphant in Versailles; and the *chinoiserie* interior walls, reminiscent of the oriental cult symbolised by the 'Porcelain Trianon' palace. This combination is precisely what a Frenchman like Laprada, who introduced Louis XIV's grand style into Portuguese sculpture, would have recommended. He was evidently eager to launch other novelties in his adopted country, such as the imitation of oriental lacquers, perhaps already tried out in Lisbon palaces that disappeared in the 1755 earthquake.

Although the Lapradian theory put forward here is now widely accepted, there are some reservations. This is shown, for example, by the question mark accompanying the attribution of the Coimbra library to Laprada in the Calouste Gulbenkian Foundation's exhibition catalogue of photographs of 17th and 18th century Portuguese architecture at the First Baroque Festival in Bahia in 1968.[81] It is also included in the catalogue of an enlarged version of the same

[80] Carvalho A. (1964). Novas revelações para a história do Barroco em Portugal. II-O mestre das gloriosas máquinas douradas da Lisboa setecentista. O artista Claude de Laprade (1682-1738). On offprint of *Belas-Artes*. 20, 50.

[81] The Baroque Festival in Bahia, 1968. The exhibition: Aspectos da Arquitectura Barroca Luso-Brasileira" was organized by the Calouste Gulbenkian Foundation, in Salvador da Bahia. https://gulbenkian.pt/historia-das-exposicoes/exhibitions/127/.

exhibition held in Braga on the occasion of the International Study Conference on "18th Century Art in Portugal", in homage to André Soares, April 1973.[82]

In 1969, in order to reduce, if not eliminate, such reservations, I decided to make a detailed examination of the architecture of Coimbra University's *Biblioteca Joanina* in relation to the known works of Claudio de Laprada. This study would highlight the many parallels that exist and, at the same time, point out the strong similarities that link the library with the three beautiful carved shutters in the Senhor das Barrocas Church, in Aveiro.[83] Begun in 1722, this is another work attributable to Claudio de Laprada.

Such a stylistic analysis is one of the aims of this book. Another is to publish, for the first time, the documentation found in the *Arquivo Distrital de Coimbra* (Coimbra District Archive) related to the construction of this majestic building, as well as to do justice to the extraordinary figure of Gaspar[84]Ferreira, Coimbra architect, carver and master builder of the university. A further aim was the study of the roles played by the two great Lisbon painters, António Simões Ribeiro and Manuel da Silva, in this work at Coimbra. For this task, I had the good fortune to find unpublished documents of great interest. My plan also includes gathering various types of monuments, linked by their relationship with the Coimbra library. Ultimately, in putting this book together I wanted to reveal to the public the total beauty of the building in all its complex and original grandeur, as the outstanding work of the equally rich, noble and complex style that, for want of a better one, bears the name of King João V.

---

[82] Robert C. Smith refers to Actas do congresso: A arte em Portugal no século XVIII (1973). *Bracara Augusta*, 64.

[83] About the Senhor das Barrocas Church, in Aveiro, see Pimentel, H. (2018) - *Plantas centralizadas na cidade de Aveiro: a Capela do Senhor das Barrocas (1722 - 1732)*. (Master's dissertation in Architecture, Faculdade de Ciências e Tecnologia da Universidade de Coimbra).

[84] In the original, certainly by mistake, 'Gabriel'.

Notes

1) This bibliographic reference should refer to Braga, T. (1892-1902) - *História da Universidade de Coimbra nas suas relações com a instrução pública*. Academia Real das Ciências.

2) "The library, which is one of the most magnificent works of art in the kingdom, has just been completed to perfection."[85], in Francisco Carneiro de Figueiroa, F.C. (1937) - *Memórias da Universidade de Coimbra*. (p. 164). Imprensa da Universidade de Coimbra, p. 164.

3) Atanazi Rackzinski, ***Les arts en Portugal: lettres adressées a la société artistique et scientifique de Berlin et accompagnées de documents*** **Paris, 1846, p. 471.**

[85] In the original: "Acabou-se de fazer com toda a perfeiçaõ a caza da Livraria que he huma das mais magnificas obras que tem este Reyno". Translator´s note.

I – History and Construction

Coimbra University was unique among 18th century peninsular universities in having its own new, monumental building for its library. Authorized by João V in 1716, this splendid structure replaced the modest facilities of the late 15th and early 16th century, which are the first recorded in the university's history. (1)

According to António José Teixeira, the first reference to Coimbra University library is contained in a provision from João III, from 17th June 1541, addressed to the dean, D. Bernardo da Cruz. (2) In this document, the king orders that the dean consult with the receiver of the university rents, Nicolau Leitão, who had brought the library's books from Lisbon in 1537, when, after 160 years of being in the capital, the university returned to its former seat in Coimbra. By the instructions of this provision, the dean should choose the best place "from the rooms of its palaces"[86] for the books, whose shelves had been authorized by another provision on the same date sent to Nicolau Leitão. (3)

There is nothing known, however, about this first installation, which must have been small and probably provisional. In 1573, the foundation of a library was recommended by D. Ayres da Silva, elected Bishop of Porto, (4) who, in his quality of university visitor and reformer, revealed that King Sebastião of Portugal wanted a library and a hospital there. (5) Yet nothing was done until 1597, when the

[86] In the original: "d´entre as divisões dos seus paços". Translator's note.

statutes of the university were published and declared that "There will be a public library in the University, with all the books from all Faculties on shelves or in cabinets held by chains; divided and organized, in the best way possible". [87] (6)

On 28th October of the same year, Dean Afonso Furtado de Mendonça (7) ordered "a house for a library"[88], naming, at the same time, Pedro Mariz, Bachelor of Canon Law, as its library-keeper. (8) A famous writer, he bought books for the new library in Venice and other foreign cities. (9) In the middle of the last century,[89] the university historian, Florêncio Mago Barreto Feio, said that this 'house' would probably have been located "under the *Via Latina* or on the lower floor of the *Paços,* on the Rua do Norte side".[90] In other words, its location was insignificant. (10)

The whole of the 17th century passed with few references to the library, which remained an unimportant matter. There is a provision dated from 12th February, 1624, in Lisbon, however, that mentions the death of the library-keeper, Francisco Vazi. (11) On 20th July of the following year, a royal letter ordered a revision of the library by Father João Alves Troco, to collect some curiosities from it. (12) Similarly, João IV, writing from Alcântara on 23rd April 1651, instructed the Dean, Manuel de Saldanha, (13) to show the library to L. F. Tresendorf, a Swede "that was going to visit Coimbra".[91] (14) A provision from Afonso VI, from 27th August 1677, commissioned the works needed on the library and authorised the spending of 118$00 for the

---

[87] In the original: "Averá na Universidade huma libraria publica, na qual estarão os livros de todas as faculdades em estantes ou almarios presos por cadeas, e repartidos e ordenados, na melhor maneira, e ordem que puder ser para bom conserto". Translator's note.

[88] In the original: "uma caza para livraria". Translator´s note.

[89] Robert C. Smith refers to 19th century.

[90] In the original: "por baixo da Via Latina ou, em parte do andar inferior dos paços pelo lado da Rua do Norte". Translator's note.

[91] In the original: "que iria visitar Coimbra". Translator's note.

Fig. 7 D. Nuno da Silva Teles. UCP (Private Examination room)

purpose. (15) At the end of the 17th century, the major works of D. Nuno da Silva Teles (16) were undertaken and gave the University the *Pátio dos Estudos Gerais de Teologia* (General Theology Studies Courtyard) and the *Casa do Exame Privado* (Private Examination Room), without enlarging the library. (17) So, it is not surprising that Father António Carvalho da Costa, when publishing the second volume of his work on Portuguese chorography in 1708, makes no special mention of the university library, which was just one of the "many" that Coimbra then had. (18) António José Teixeira located its modest home on the right of the *Porta Férrea* (Iron Gate)[92] on the first floor of the *Paço das Escholas* (Faculties' Courtyard).[93] (19)

The solution was found in 1716 by the powerful Dean Nuno da Silva Teles, nephew of another of the same name, censor and secretary of the *Academia Real da História Portuguesa* (Royal Academy of Portuguese History), member of the Holy Inquisition and Chaplain of Honour.[94] (20) After addressing João V, Protector of the University (21), the Dean was not only given royal approval for the purchase of the private library of Francisco Barreto and the increase of the annual budget for buying books, from 40$00 to 100$00 *reis*; but also the remarkable authorization to build "a house suitable for a book room (...) for the existing one is small and dark".[95] (22)

These permits, perhaps inspired by Filipe V of Spain's decision to found a royal library in Madrid in 1712, together with the veneration João V had for his father King Pedro II's role as Protector of

---

[92] In the original: "Porta Férrea". Translator's note.

[93] In the original: "Paço das Escolas". Translator's note.

[94] Officer of the Portuguese Royal Household. Chosen from among the kingdom's most important prelates of noble backgrounds. The *sumilher da cortina* was responsible for drawing the Royal Chapel gallery curtain as the king entered for divine office. He was also tasked with removing the dust guard from the king›s kneeler for his prayers.

[95] In the original: "uma caza competente para huma boa livraria (...) por ser pequena e escura a caza que servia áquelle ministerio". Translator's note.

Coimbra University, were granted by the provision of 31st October 1716. The institution was thus granted the right "to make a house in the mentioned place [the courtyard of the University] where it would be useful and less expensive".[96] (24)

The document does not deal with how the building is to be financed, but the royal authorization implied the king's donation of the necessary money to the university. This money going into the university chest, so often mentioned in its account books, started immediately to be paid to the constructors of the new building, from spring 1717. It is at this time that the payment lists begin to appear and continue until 1728, during the deanships of Pedro Sanches Farinha de Beana (25) and Francisco Carneiro de Figueiroa, his successor. (26)

The masonry works started officially on 17th July 1717, in the presence of Dean Silva Teles and a great number of university teachers. (27)

It was only on 14th August, almost a month afterwards, that a contract for the construction was drawn up and signed with João Carvalho Ferreira, "masonry master living in Cellas outside the walls of this town".[97] (28) This document informs us that, besides pricing the different types of masonry and stonework to be used in building the library, "he spent many days in this city and its public places, as well as in the courtyard of the university itself, looking for those who would do the work for less than the prices in the original estimates.[98]

According to the information on the contract, Master João Carvalho Ferreira, who had agreed to do the work for "35.000 *reis* less than

---

[96] In the original: "Hey por bem, mandeis fazer a dita caza, no citio sobredito [pátio da Universidade] como mais útil, e de menos despeza (...). Translator's note. The quote by Robert Smith was not precise: "para no pateo desta Universidade se fazer uma casa para a livraria no sitio onde seja util e de menos despeza". We review it.

[97] In the original: "mestre-de-obras de pedraria morador ao Burgo de Cella extra muros desta Cidade". Translator's note.

[98] In the original: "andara muitos dias a pregam por esta dita cidade e lugares públicos della e no terreiro da mesma universidade para se arrematar às pessoas ou pessoa que na dita obra quisessem lançar por menos dos preços que estauam nos apontamentos que se fizeram para a dita obra". Translator's note.

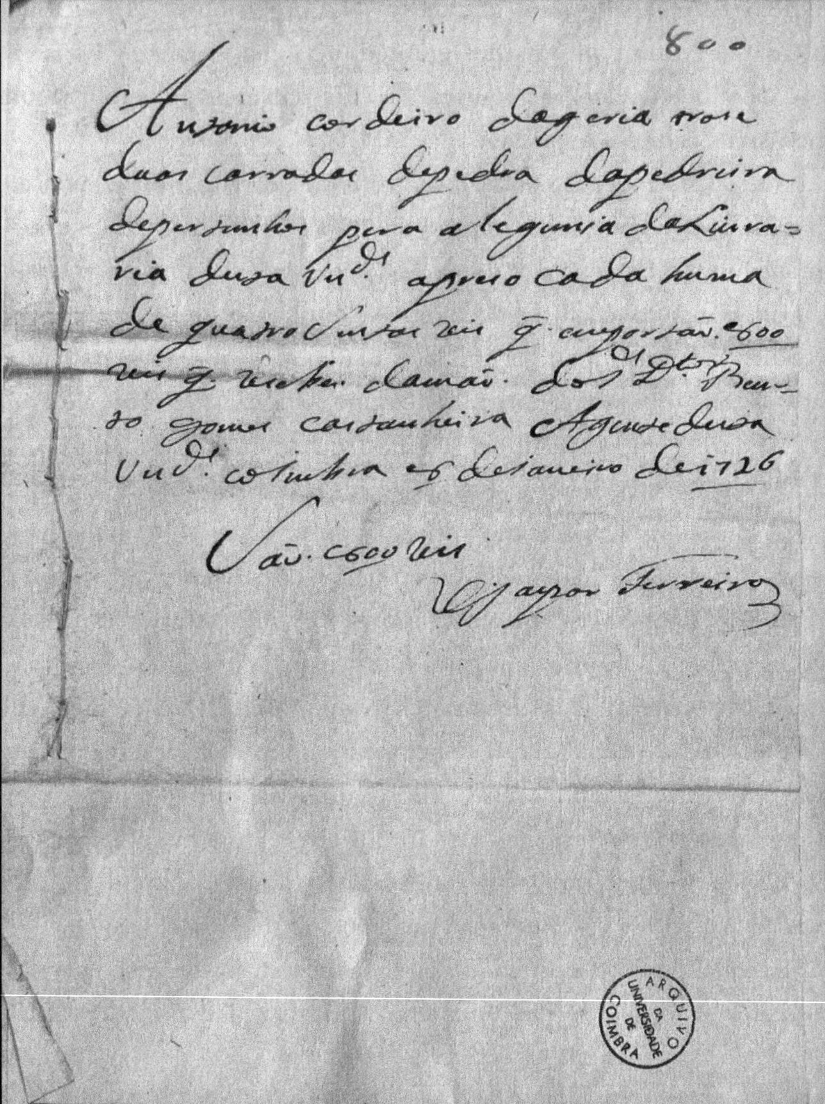

800

Antonio cordeiro da geria trose
duas carradas de pedra da pedreira
de persumhos pera a leguaria da Livraria desta Univ.de a preço cada huma
de quatro sentos reis q. emportão 800
reis q. recebeo da mão do S.r D.r Bento gomes cardanheira Agente desta
Univ.de coimbra 2 de Janeiro de 1726

São 800 reis

Mayor Ferreira

Figs. 8 and 9. Payrolls for artists working in the Library

Esta he a conta das pedras q̃ consta dos livros por ellas ter entregue o dito Cabouqueiro Antonio Luis Vilhena.

Estas pedras me consta q̃ ja vierão e tambem a alquitrava — O mesmo Cabouq.ro diz q̃ neste anno virão mais duas pedras que alinçou por sua conta, q̃ ainda lhe não estão carregadas no Lo.o, e consta de ser assim se veria a grandeza das ditas pedras p.a conforme a ella se lhe pagar o seu lanço.

E com a importancia destas pedras, e a conta de cola sima ajuste o Almoxarife a sua conta com este Cabouq.ro, e trata de satisfazer o q̃ lhe estiver devendo, advertindo q̃ ainda está na pred.te sua verga do portal, e q̃ o dito Cabouq.ro deve dar conta.

E q.to as 3. colunas q̃ o mesmo Cabouq.ro alinçou deve seguir-se a mesma da Fazenda, q̃ lhe mande pagar o dito a lanço por conta do Mestre João de Carv.o por lhe dar as medidas das ditas colunas erradas, e não servirem por essa causa p.a a obra, e caso q̃ seja culpa do dito Cabouq.ro por não terem as colunas a medida competente deve perder o dito Cabouq.ro o seu trabalho. Soure 20 de Agosto de 1723.

[signature]

Vi este Rol. Fernando Pereira Mourão

A lauda atras importa — 130$950
It. mais do alanço das quatro pedras asima a 480 por cada huã — 001$920
It. E um bocado de dez dias q̃ o D.or Giraldo mandou dar-lhe — 000$400

Somatudo — 133$270

the original estimates"[99], was a wealthy man, the owner of several houses, vineyards and olive groves on the outskirts of Coimbra. He was also the neighbour of the widow of Manuel Fernandes, nicknamed the 'Sogeiro' who was foreman on the works of the Monastery of Santa Clara, in Coimbra. (29) The guarantor and main payer of the contract was João Rodrigues de Almeida, (30) "master carpenter of the works of this university"[100] and therefore linked to the great commission of the new 'Library House'.

Tracing its history in detail, we have contracts and payment sheets of the main artisans in the university account books. (31) There is also a complete breakdown of the weekly wages, detailing the worker's payments. This fills nine boxes in the university archives, (32) through which it is possible to create a general idea of the works' progression. Made through the order of Bento Gomes Castanheira, the university agent who served as paymaster, the workers' payments started with the preparation works that took place during the week of 4th May 1717, "with the masons and workers who are passing lime".[101] (33) A fortnight later, we have the "list of payments for the carts that will pick up the rubble, which started on 19th May and ended on 22nd of the same month".[102] (34)

On the 25th May, Manuel Gomes, the 'rent man' or university debt collector, went to place (35) "announcements in Carrima and Souzellas for tilers to come and make their pitches, where he spent a day".[103]

[99] In the original: "menos trinta e cinco mil reis dos preços que estauam nos apontamentos". Translator's note.

[100] In the original: "mestre de carpintaria das obras desta Universidade". Translator's note.

[101] In the original: "com os "laurantes e trabalhadores que andão passando a cal". Translator's note.

[102] In the original: "o rol das ferias dos carros que andarão ao entulho que começou a 19 de Maio e findou a vinte e dois deste mes". Translator's note.

[103] In the original: "escriptos em o lugar de Carrima e em Souzellas para os homens da telha virem fazer seos lanços donde gastou hum dia". Translator's note.

He performed the same task in the small villages of S. Fagundo and Lavarrabos.

Meanwhile, sand from outside Coimbra and from Lisbon arrived. (36) On 24th June, João Antunes, from Vilarinho de Lousã, sold the university "trinta e duas couseiras postas".

In the week between 17th and 24th July, when the actual inauguration of the works took place, in the presence of the Dean, the list of payments shows there was a small army of workers: carpenters and sawyers, quarrymen, masons, workers and boys, (38) attendants and women that, on a smaller scale, foreshadowed the herd of people soon to be summoned for the works at Mafra. (39)

The payment list goes on for the rest of 1717 and the first months of 1718. In March, there are the first references to the masonry stone, transported in ox carts from the quarry of João Oliveira in the region of Portunhos; and, in July, from a quarry belonging to the university in the same area, driven by a certain António Simões, from Ançã. (40) At the same time, boatmen went up the River Mondego to get wood, with one of them, Manuel Lopes from Carvoeiro do Termos, in Penacova, complaining of having made two trips to Tobim without being paid enough. (41)

In April 1718, "quantities of bricks"[104] from the *Colégio de Nossa Senhora da Graça*, of Coimbra, (42) and from Sandelgas (43) arrived at the library site. Now sawyers, carpenters and masons were working at such speed, apparently, that in the week of 18th to 25th July it was already possible to begin preparing the shelves for the library's three rooms. (44)

Several teams of carpenters and woodcarvers or 'ensemblers' (although this word is never used in the payrolls) committed themselves to this vast initiative until 23rd June 1725, under the direction of Gaspar

[104] In the original: "quantidades de tijolo". Translator's note.

Ferreira[105], from Coimbra, the foreman of the library and university works. Ferreira, called "master woodcarver", earned 500 *reis* per day; with the daily rate of the men he directed - normally four, five or six -, ranging from 120 to 300 *reis*. (45) We know the names of these craftsmen, for example, Veríssimo Correia, João de Oliveira, Manuel Marques, Álvaro da Costa, Manuel Carvalho, Caetano da Silva, Álvaro Francisco, Jacinto de Araújo, Domingos António and João Correia.

In August 1723, the woodcarver Manuel de Andrade, who lived in the small village of Torres, "undertook the contract to clean the balcony balusters of the Library of this University".[106] (46) On the 14th of September , de Andrade had completed "14 of the large balusters"[107] that "at 960 *reis* each, comes to 13,440 *reis*", and 24 small balusters at 550 *reis* each. (47)[108]. In October, he completed 25 of the large and 28 of the small; in November, 10 and 13 more; and, in April and July 1724, another 41. (48) In July, master turner Xavier Gomes finished "42 balls" for the "library balcony", which must have been the flower baskets on top of the respective pillars. (49)

Gaspar Ferreira's career, the foreman who directed the construction of the shelves from 1718 to 1725 is well documented. When he

---

[105] For more information on the work of this master architect and carver, see Alves A. (1980). Artistas e Artífices nas Dioceses de Lamego e Viseu. *Revista Beira Alta*. XXXIX, facs 3- 4, 357-367 and Alves A. (1982). A actividade de Gaspar Ferreira em terras do interior Beirão. *Mundo da Arte*. 6.

New approaches and documentation on the work of this architect have been added by Pimentel, A.F. (1989) - Gaspar Ferreira (p. 187). In José F.P. (ed.), *Dicionário da arte barroca em Portugal*. Presença. 7 and by Santos, D. S. (2013) - *Azulejaria de fabrico coimbrão (1699-1801), Artífices e artistas. Cronologia. Iconografia* (pp. 227-232). (PhD Thesis in Portuguese Art History, presented at the Faculty of Letters of the University of Porto). I. Miguel Portela (Jan-Feb. 2020), in the article O mestre de obras de arquitetura Gaspar Ferreira e o convento dos dominicanos da Batalha published in *Jornal da Golpilheira*, adds one more piece of information on this artist's work.

[106] In the original: "que tomou de empreitada a limpeza dos balaustres da baranda da Livraria desta Universidade". Translator's note.

[107] In the original: "dos balaustres grandes quatorze". Translator's note.

[108] We altered the date on Smith´s text for it mentioned the month of September for the beginning of the work and in the original document the date is 23rd August.

Fig. 10 Church of Mercy. Mangualde. Portugal. Gaspar Ferreira
@ Fátima Eusébio

Fig. 11 Choir stall of the Viseu Cathedral. Portugal. Gaspar Ferreira
@ Fátima Eusébio

died, on 20th October 1762, he was, according to the parish priest of S. João da Cruz of Coimbra, 73 years old. This means he must have been born around 1689. (50) The death certificate also shows that Gaspar Ferreira married twice: first to Violante Teixeira and then to Joaquina Luísa. Although there are no records of children or professions in this document, his first wife was called "wife of Gaspar Ferreira, woodcarver" in 1720. (51)

Performing the allied crafts as "master architect" and "master woodcarver", Ferreira designed and executed both altarpieces and other woodcarvings, as well as being responsible for some buildings in the *Beiras* region. His first known work was directing the construction of the 'Library House' shelves.[109] In 1721, he designed the plan "for the stonework" of the Santa Casa da Misericórdia Church, in Mangualde. (52) A picturesque building, with a heavy, rough style, most of the expenses were paid by a local nobleman, Simão Pais do Amaral, ancestor of the counts of Anadia and director of the Santa Casa.

In the same year, Gaspar Ferreira made "two plans for the organ base and columns" for Viseu Cathedral in a box that has since been lost. (53)

In 1725, his name is shown in the contract of Alexandre de Castro and José Rodrigues to do the stone and carpentry works for the main chapel of the Alvorge Church sacristy, according to the notes made "by the foreman of the University works, Gaspar Ferreira". (54) This was one of the parish churches belonging to Coimbra University. In 1727, he signed a contract to finish the interior of the area underneath the rooms of the university library, and to make a Tenebrae hearse in imitation of the one in Coimbra Cathedral, his

[109] Diana Gonçalves dos Santos suggests this took place in 1713, the year in which Gaspar Ferreira was named in the notarial contract for the execution of the high altar of the S. Salvador Church, in Coimbra. The carving was commissioned by João de Azevedo. AUC - *Fundo Notarial de Coimbra*. Tabelião Francisco Gomes Pinheiro. Dep.V; Sec.I-Es; Est.9; Tab.4; No.25, pp.15-16. Cf. Santos, D.G. *op. cit.*, (p. 230).

guarantor being the carpenter Sebastião Rodrigues, who worked on the shelves. (55) Soon after, on 24th January 1728, Ferreira signed another contract for a non-specified work, which might have been restoration work on the *Porta Férrea* (Iron Gate), the entrance to the university courtyard. (56) The guarantor was Manuel Carvalho, another woodworker at the library. In the same year, Gaspar Ferreira designed the new bell tower, in the NW corner of the courtyard, for which received 6.400 *reis*. (57) The drafts sent to Lisbon were rejected in favour of another scheme made by a royal architect, (58) probably the Roman, António Canevari.[110] (59)

At the same time, it was settled that Gaspar Ferreira, as "foreman of the University" would oversee the construction of this tower, (60) which lasted until the beginning of 1733. (61) He received a wage of 600 *reis* per day, "with the proviso that he could miss only one to two days a week". He also designed the four faces of the clock tower, executed by Verissimo da Veiga, from the small town of Condeixa. (62) In the meantime, Gaspar Ferreira practised his craft of woodcarver, designing the altarpiece of the main chapel with "the two niches" for the Santa Maria do Rabaçal Church. (63) On 29th July 1729, da Veiga signed a contract, which also covered designs for wood sculptures by Manuel de Andrade who, seven years before, had "cleaned" or finished the balusters for the balconies of the library shelves.

In 1731, Gaspar Ferreira received 16.800 *reis* from the *Cabido de Viseu* "for the work he had to come do and revise on the altar-piece of the main chapel of our cathedral", (64) built by Francisco Machado, from Landim. (65) The design was by the great woodcarver from Lisbon, Santos Pacheco de Lima, who also designed the new

[110] On the construction of the tower, under Canevari's design, see Pimentel, A.F. (2005). António Canevari e a torre da Universidade de Coimbra (pp. 49-58). In Natália, M. F-A. (ed.) - *Artistas e Artífices e a sua mobilidade no mundo de expressão portuguesa: actas do VII Colóquio Luso-Brasileiro de História da Arte.*

altarpiece for Porto Cathedral. (66)[111] It is hardly strange, therefore, that Ferreira returned to Viseu from September 1731 until November 1732, to make a magnificent choir stall in the main chapel of the cathedral, two wood carved credence tables and the "feet for two tables of foreign stone for the sacristy (...) of blackwood".[112] (67) The choir stalls were inspired by those of Porto Cathedral, made in 1726-27 by Manuel Marques, following the design of the eminent Porto woodcarver, Luís Pereira da Costa, (68) who made altarpieces, (69) credence tables (70) and sculpted stonework (71) for the Santa Casa da Misericórdia Church, in Mangualde. The plans for the *Recolhimento of Nossa Senhora da Conceição* (Retreat of Our Lady of the Conception) of this satellite town of Viseu, dated 1732, are also attributed to Gaspar Ferreira. The pulpits of Viseu Cathedral, whose balusters are based on those of the balconies of Coimbra University library can be also attributed to him.

As far as architecture is concerned, this *homme à tout faire*[113] served in 1737 as foreman of the works in the old cloister of the Franciscan convent of Santa Clara of Coimbra, planned, according to tradition, by the military engineer Carlos Mardel. (72) Again, in 1761, he played the same role in the construction of the convent's reception building, a whimsical rocaille-style work. (73) There are also some suggestions of this French style in the windows and door frames of the Hospital of the Santa Casa da Misericórdia Hospital in Montemor-o-Velho, which dates from 1752-54. (74) A 19th century

[111] Regarding Santos Pacheco's role in the design of the main chapel of Porto Cathedral, see Ferreira-Alves, N.M. (2001) - *A escola de talha portuense e a sua influência no norte de Portugal.* (p. 79). Edições Inapa. and Ferreira S. (2002) - *A talha dourada do altar-mor da igreja de Santa Catarina, em Lisboa. A intervenção do entalhador Santos Pacheco.* (Master's dissertation on History of Art presented at the Lusíada University of Lisbon).

[112] In the original: "os pes para duas mesas de pedra estrangeira para a sacristia (...) de pau preto". Translator's note.

[113] In French in the original. Translator´s note.

author also attributes the basic plan of the Santa Casa da Misericórdia Church in Santa Comba Dão to him. (75)[114]

With both the library and Coimbra University having been built on a foothill, it is logical to assume that the first years of their construction were spent making the walls of the substructure. In August 1719, the payment lists show the first information regarding the façades at the entry courtyard level in the "bill for the stone that the quarryman, António Luís o Botas was contracted to buy from the Outil quarry"[115]:

"2 stones for the frontispiece at 480	4$800
One stone for the top of the arches	$480
One lintel for the large windows	$480 (...)
One thick stone for a frieze	$600 (...)
8 stones for pillows at 480	3$860 (...)
25 stones for the cymbal at 350	8$750
2 door jams for the portal and two lintels for the same portal at two gold coins each and two more coins for another door jamb that broke during the transportation.	
The total sum being	48$000"

The bill from 20th [116]August 1719 (76) contains other items and shows a total of 130$950. It represents the starting point for construction on the part of the building containing the main rooms, dated 4th March 1719. This confirms the theory that the following curious complaint from one of the workers is another reference to

[114] See Pimentel, A.F. Gaspar Ferreira (...), p. 187 and Miguel Portela. O mestre de obras de arquitetura Gaspar Ferreira e o convento dos dominicanos da Batalha (...).

[115] In the original: "Conta da pedra que arricou (sic) por empreitada na pedreira de Outil o caboqueiro Antonio Luis o Botas". Translator's note.

[116] We have corrected it to date that appears on the original document. Smith's text refers to the date of 16 August.

Gaspar Ferreira. The document says that "Manuel Gonsalves Correya, from the borough of Santa Clara, was obliged to go with his pair of oxen to transport the second column for the porch of the library of this university under the charge of Gaspar Ferreira. On the third day, one of the oxen fell under the weight of the stones in such a way that it broke its teeth, not being able to eat, and for two days the claimant was at home giving it medicine to see if it could eat".[117]

In the following years of 1719, 1720, 1721 the lists of stoneworkers continue. There are also the accounts of the master locksmith Bernardo Viela that, on 22nd May 1722, made "fourteen more clamps for the security of the medallion of the Library´s portal of this University that weigh 103 *arrates*[118] that at sixty *reis* each makes a total of 7,210 *reis*".[119] We therefore know that, nearly two and a half years after the transportation of the columns, the library's large entrance door was almost finished.

Although no reference is made to the roofs, the library must have been covered and the ceilings of the three large rooms installed long before 22nd June 1723, when its paintings were commissioned from António Simões Ribeiro and the gilding from Vicente Nunes "paint masters living in the city of Lisbon in the parish of S. Nicolau".[120]

---

[117] In the original: "Dis Manuel Golsalves Correya, do Burgo de Santa Clara que elle obrigado por notificação foy com a sua junta de Bois a condusão da segunda coluna para o pórtico da livraria desta Universidade a que foi por condutor o Mestre Gaspar Ferreira e no terseiro dia da iornada hum Boi da sua iunta cahio com o pezo da Pedra em tal forma que cahio e quebrou os dentes sem poder comer que para isso esteve o supplicante em caza dois dias fazendo Medicamentos a ver se podia comer". Translator's note. The document goes on making considerations about the evaluation of the cattle that were carrying the stones for the construction of the Library and how to proceed in their evaluation and reimbursement to the owners of the animals, in case of irreparable injuries to them.

[118] This is an ancient weight of 16 ounces, which is equivalent to 459 grammes.

[119] In the original: "mais quatorze gatos para a segurança da targe do portal da Livraria desta Universidade que pesaram cento e tres arrates que a sessenta reis emporta sete mil e duzentos e des reis". Translator's note.

[120] In the original: "mestres pintores e moradores na cidade de Lisboa na freguesia de Sam Nicolau". Translator's note.

(79) And soon after, on 28th August of the same year, the painter Manuel da Silva was contracted to paint the shelves and balconies. (80) The ceilings were finished in April 1724, while the painting of the shelves and gild work was only completed in April 1727. (81)

There is some information regarding Manuel da Silva's work[121] in Coimbra and Viseu where, like Gaspar Ferreira, he worked. He was from Lisbon and entered the S. Lucas Brotherhood, a painters' association based in the capital city, on 18th October 1706. The document that concerns him does not mention his age or address, but we know him as the son of Manuel Mendes de Ataíde and his wife, Josefa da Conceição. This information was given to the priest of Coimbra Cathedral when, on 15th March 1710, Manuel da Silva married Jerónima Teles, also from Lisbon, in Santa Clara "outside of this town".[122] (83) After a decade of silence, we find the painter involved in a series of works for Old Coimbra Cathedral, from 1720 until 1724, for which he was paid 662$800 *reis*. (84) These activities, the result of the long vacant state of the Coimbra Diocese Cathedral, from 1717 until 1739, when the cathedral chapter could spend its income freely, correspond (more modestly) to Nicolau Nasoni and his associates' work, from 1717 to 1739, for the Porto cathedral chapter, also without a prelate. (85) Unlike what happened in the city of the Douro, however, the results seem to have been completely lost in the successive "restorations" of the late Romanesque-Gothic Coimbra Cathedral.

These works of Manuel da Silva are divided in many categories. He silvered and gilded several candlesticks, torches, vases, pelmets and lamps, and painted the "sepulchre" of the Cathedral's Holy Week

---

[121] On the life and work of Manuel da Silva, complementing Smith's information and placing the career of this master painter in the broader horizon of collaborations with other artists, see Pimentel, A.F. (1996) - Manuel da Silva e a difusão do barroco nas Beiras (pp. 428-455). *Oficinas regionais. Actas do VI simpósio luso-espanhol de história da arte*. Instituto Politécnico de Tomar and Santos, D.G. *op. cit.* (pp. 241-256).

[122] In the original: "de fora desta cidade". Translator's note.

gold and white. He plastered some ceilings, perhaps for paintings and "varnished" various pieces of furniture, including a new section of the stalls, certain safes, chests and confessionals, a group of buffets, including ten "in black", imitating ebony. In the chapter room and the cloisters, he painted doors, windows and railings green, the favourite colour for these kinds of architectural features. In the process, eleven doors were given a pretence of the "colour of Angelim", the most commonly used Brazilian wood for doors and windows in the richest 18th century monasteries and churches.

At the same time, Manuel da Silva practised the art of *charoar*, the imitation of oriental lacquers, on several picture frames, boards and other woodwork, spread throughout the cathedral chapter's chambers. We can cite nine frames "with their fillets and acanthus leaves" and a niche, in which he painted two cypresses. (86)

Portraits and other kinds of painting were also done for the Coimbra Canon. Manuel da Silva made seven portraits of prelates and, for the chapter house, four of unidentified pontiffs and one of the "last Pope", (87) together with four panels of fruit still lifes or *bodegones*. For the choir of Coimbra Cathedral, Manuel da Silva portrayed the four Evangelists. He painted also no less than 19,803 glazed tiles for the two chapter houses, three flights of the cloister and its staircase, which have now all disappeared. (88) As he worked together with Agostinho Paiva[123], Coimbra's best-known potter of this period, (89) it is possible that this kind of ceramic was the so-called *albarrada*, with vases or baskets of flowers between pairs of small animals or attached birds. This was the pattern used by Paiva in the grand cladding of the *Gerais* Courtyard and the university's Private Examination Room, completed in 1701-1702. (90) Similar designs are

[123] The most recent studies on Agostinho de Paiva have been by Santos, D.G. *op. cit.* (pp. 220-240) and Pais, A.N., Pacheco A. and Coroado J. (2007) - *Cerâmica de Coimbra: do século XVI-XX*. INAPA.

Fig. 12 Cartouche surmounted by a royal crown.
Joanine Library. © Nuno Antunes

Fig. 13 Detail of a bookcase decoration in Coimbra's Joanine Library.

to be found on the corridors and cloisters of the former Augustinian *Sapiência* (Wisdom) Convent, in Coimbra (91), and also at the former College of *Santo António da Pedreira*, in the same city. (92) Similar decoration is to be seen on the "grotesque" (93) tiles of the upper cloister of Viseu Cathedral, named in the payment provision of 23rd March 1724, in favour of Manuel da Silva. (94) Working again with Agostinho de Paiva (95), da Silva and he must have repeated here what they accomplished in the lost works of the Coimbra chapter. (96)

Six months before this date, Manuel da Silva had entered the service of Coimbra University, signing the contract on 28th August 1723, for "the gilding of the three houses, as well the ceiling of the house of the mentioned oratory at a price of one hundred *reis*".[124] (97) The contract continues establishing the rhythm of the payments and specifying that the work on the oratory should be finished before 8th October 1723. Through the university account books, we know that on 6th November 1723, Manuel da Silva, "master painter", received 100$00 *reis* for "the gilding work of the chapel of the houses of the Dean of this University and the painting of the ceiling of the house of the mentioned oratory".[125] (98) On 1st April 1724, the same amount was given to him, "for the painting in perspective of the oratory in the dean's residence[126]. (99) This was probably, as we will see, the first attempt made in Coimbra of imitating Italian *quadratura*, brought to Portugal a dozen years before by the Tuscan painter, Vicenzo Bacherelli, (99) with whom Manuel da Silva might have studied in Lisbon.

From 4th December 1723, (100) there is news about payments made to Manuel da Silva for the painting and gilding, "with all grace and

---

124 In the original: "o douramento das tres cazas e asim mais o douramento do oratorio das cazas do senhor Reitor desta Universidade e a pintura do teto da caza do dito oratorio em presso de sem mil *reis* (...)". Translator's ´note.

125 In the original: "obra do douramento da capella das Cazas do Senhor Reitor desta Universidade e pintura do tecto da caza do dito oratorio". Translator's note.

126 In the original: "pella pintura de perspectiva do oratório das cazas do Senhor Reitor". Translator's note.

care",[127] (101) of the "library bookshelves", as well as the medallions of the faculties topping the arches of the three majestic rooms, and other details. Therefore, he worked here contemporaneously to his activity in the Dean's houses, using the type of painting called then *charão* in Portugal and 'japanning' in England, from where it may have come to the Lusitanian centres. 'Japanning' consists of small landscapes or decorative groups with a finish imitating the oriental lacquers. (102) This kind of *chinoiserie* had already been done by Manuel da Silva in his painting and gilding of Viseu Cathedral's upper choir and pipe organ, paid for on 4th August 1721. (103) The vast work on the library, which would last three and a half years, seems to have excluded the painter from other university services.

These, however, were resumed in 1727, soon after the library interior was finished, with da Silva painting 86 'flower sticks' on the walls or ceiling of the room called *Actos Grandes*, or *Capelos,* called in the document *Sala dos Reis,*[128] because of the portraits of sovereigns lining the top part of its walls. (104) At the same time, Manuel da Silva painted the choir of the university chapel green, and the old organ case 'verdigris',[129] "inside and out", together with "some big cabinets"[130] and other pieces of furniture, now all replaced.

Still in 1727, Manuel da Silva, then living in Rua da Moeda, in the parish of S. João da Cruz, where he died a decade later, replaced the painter Gabriel Rodrigues, who "had little perfection in the art",[131] in the important undertaking of gilding the main chapel of Santa Clara, the royal convent of Franciscan nuns, to paint its ceiling "all grotesque" and gild the pulpit, for 340.000 *reis.* (106)

---

[127] In the original: "com toda a galhardia e primor". Translator's note.

[128] In the original: "Sala dos reis". Translator's note.

[129] In the original: "Verdete". Translator's note.

[130] In the original: "huns almarios grandes". Translator's note.

[131] In the original: "tinha pouca perfeição da arte". Translator's note.

Fig. 14 Glass panes of Coimbra's Joanine Library before the 1943-45 restoration. CFT001.12359. Legado Robert Chester Smith, Fundação Calouste Gulbenkian, Biblioteca de Arte e Arquivos, Lisboa.

The gilding of the "paschal candle torch"[132] and the painting of Tenebrae hearse and doors of the market's butchers date from the following year. (107) In 1731, Manuel da Silva gilded and painted the back and niche of the chapel's sacristy chest. (108) Dating from 1694, (109) no traces of this work remain today.

News of Manuel da Silva comes to a stop here. His career evidently ended with the paintings done for the university between 1723 and 1727. He was replaced in the university service by Gabriel Pereira da Cunha, born in Ponte da Morcela and living in Rua das Covas, Coimbra. (110) In 1728 (111) and 1733, (112) da Cunha gilded university church altarpieces. On 1st June 1737, (113) when Manuel da Silva died, Gabriel Pereira was contracted to gild and paint the new pipe organ case at the royal chapel of Coimbra University, built in 1732, under the direction of Gaspar Ferreira.

On 14th December 1722, André Salgado, a glassworker also living in Rua das Covas, was contracted at the price of one *tostão* per span (22 cm, or 8 inches), to "make all the panes necessary for the Library windows and for all parts that are necessary for the mentioned Library (...) in the form of other windowpanes that are in the University".[133] (114) On 30th April 1723, moreover, Bernardo Vieira presented his bill for "112 irons for the four windows of the middle house to hold the windowpanes".[134] (115) In 1724, while Gaspar Ferreira and his carvers finished the library bookshelves, a new locksmith called Manuel Francisco handed in "two hooks for the two windows, for the wire nets that each one has".[135] (116)

---

[132] In the original: "tocheira do sírio pascal". Translator's note.

[133] In the original: "fazer todas as uidrasas que forem neseçarias para as ginellas da Caza da Liuraria e pera todas as mais partes que forem neseçarias na dita Caza da Liuraria...na forma das mais uidrasas que estão na universidade". Translator's note.

[134] In the original: "112 ferros pera as quatro janelas da casa do meyo pera segurar as vidraças". Translator's note.

[135] In the original: Dois emvestidores para duas janelas, para as redes de arame que cada huma tem". Translator's note.

Fig. 15 Floor of the Joanine Library. CFT001.12386. Legado Robert Chester Smith, Fundação Calouste Gulbenkian, Biblioteca de Arte e Arquivos, Lisboa.

Fig. 16 Library's hardware
© Sílvia Ferreira

Six months after, on 10th February 1725, Albano dos Reis Salgado presented his bill of 45$440 *reis* regarding several windowpanes and the respective nails, at the same time informing those concerned about the death of his father, the glassworker whom he had replaced. (117)

On 23rd June, the last payment to the carvers was made, (118) while the carpenters, under the direction of Master Manuel Carvalho, worked until the end of the year. (119)

The locksmith Manuel Francisco delivered several hinges, locks and their plates and holdfasts for the wire nets, made by João Carvalho "official tinsmith of this City".[136] (120) His contract, dated 16th September 1724, also calls Carvalho "master glassworker resident in this city in Rua de Curuche",[137] declaring that he had been awarded "the nets for the windows of the Library House of this University at the price of forty *reis* for each handspan of iron wire, which is called the best mesh, made with the measurements given by Master Gaspar Ferreira".[138] (121) In his petition of 10th November 1725, concerning the nets, he states that "having made four already placed, there is now another one ready to place".[139] (122) He wanted more money to buy wire.

On 14th July 1725, the loaders Francisco de Figueiredo and Francisco Gonçalves requested payment for four loads of *pedra parda,*[140] from Portunhos, for the floors of the three main library rooms. (123) The invoice of Bento Luís and Bartolomeu Pinheiro, quarrymen from Portunhos, who brought thirty-two loads for the

---

[136] In the original: "oficial de latoeiro desta Cidade". Translator's note.

[137] In the original: "mestre vidraceiro e morador nesta cidade na Rua de Curuche della". Translator's note.

[138] In the original: "as redes pera as ginellas da caza da Liuraria desta universidade em preço cada palmo de rede de quarenta reis feita de arame de ferro a que chamão da melhor feita a malha pella medida que deu o mestre Gaspar Ferreira (...)". Translator's note.

[139] In the original: "tem feito já coatro que se achão assentadas, e agora se acha com outra finda que esta prompta para se assentar (...)". Translator´s note.

[140] A yellowish/brown stone. Translator´s note.

Fig. 17 Portrait of D. Luís da Cunha,
in *Memórias da Paz de Utrech oferecidas a El Rey N. S. por D. Luís da*
nha seu embaixador. In https://purl.pt/23773/1/index.html#/13/htm

Fig. 18 Cardinal da Mota coat of arms https://purl.pt/12417/2/

same purpose is dated September of the same year, and António Cordeiro would deliver two more in November. (124)

The last stones for the flooring are dated January 1726 (125) and the last hooks for the library in February. (126) Meanwhile, the lower area – the last stage of the construction of the Joanine Library – entrusted to Master Gaspar Ferreira by contract on 2nd December, 1727, (127) was being completed. Once again, the carpenter Sebastião Rodrigues, who had worked on the bookshelves, appears as guarantor.

Perhaps based on this documentation, Florêncio Barreto Feio concluded that the library building was finished in 1728. (128) Bernardo de Brito Botelho, however, writing of the Capelos Room in around 1734, stated "it is hoped that the magnificence of the Library is finally finished, in order to make this royal room longer".[141] (129) In fact, several details were missing.

In February 1729, the tinsmith João da Costa received 33$700 *reis* "for the remaining signs for the library doors".[142] (130) This artist was probably the same João da Costa "master tinsmith resident in Rua de Cruche" who, in 1724, had made "a brass imperial crown and sphere for the figure that is on this University Library staircase".[143] (131) He was to reappear, on 8th March, 1733, to complete the last part of "the Library nets and other things",[144] (132) substituting, as it seems, Master João Carvalho: he was paid only 8$240 *reis*. 12th April 1742 is the date of 24$000 *reis* being paid to the Coimbra painter, José de Sousa, "for the gilding of the ironwork of the Library door".[145] (133) Other things undoubtedly included

---

[141] In the original: "se espera se acabe de todo, a magnificência da Livraria, para se fazer esta Regia Salla, mais comprida (...)". Translator´s note.

[142] In the original: "do resto dos letreiros para as portas da Livraria". Translator´s note.

[143] In the original: "huma croa emperial e huma esfera de latam para a figura que esta na escada da Livraria desta Universidade". Translator's note.

[144] In the original: "redes da Livraria e outras cousas". Translator's note.

[145] In the original: "que elle dourou toda a ferragem da porta da Caza da livraria desta Universidade". Translator's note.

João da Costa's sign plate, the thick nails and maybe the "two golden *Gualdras* (sic) and two of the university library's escutcheons".[146] These must have been the knocker and the handle and escutcheon given to Gaspar Ferreira, in 1728, in his capacity as master builder, by João Carvalho, who asked him to be paid 4$400 *reis*, "because he is a poor man and needs this sum of money".[147] (134)

Meanwhile, overspending in his usual manner, João V used his diplomatic envoys in several European courts to acquire whole libraries, like that of the poet, humanist and Jesuit preacher, Charles de la Rue, in Paris in 1725. (135) In the following years of 1726 and 1727, the diplomat Luís da Cunha (136) researched large English and Belgian libraries, taking notes and making drafts, now apparently lost. (137) Old manuscripts came from London (138) and, in 1729 and 1730, almost four *contos de reis* were given to Cardinal Mota for the purchase of books, probably in Rome. (139) Two other envoys were dispatched to Amsterdam with the same purpose. (140)

However, despite all these efforts, it seems that in 1741 the Library was still devoid of books. (141) The annual budget of 100$00 *reis* for their purchase, occasionally doubled, was maintained until 1750 (142) when, at the end of his long reign, João V made it known through his provision of 8th April "I hereby declare that from the University's surplus income, another fifty thousand cruzados be spent on Books for the said Library".[148] (143)

Without revealing his sources, Barreto Feio estimated the total construction and decoration expenses of the Coimbra University library to be 66,622$129 *reis*. (144) As high as the sum might seem,

---

[146] In the original: duas Gualdras (sic) e dois escudetes para as portas da Livraria da Universidade douradas". Translator's note.

[147] In the original: "porque he homem pobre e nessessitta do emporte". Translator's note.

[148] In the original: "Hey por bem que dos sobejos das rendas da Universidade se empreguem mais sincoenta mil cruzados em Livros para a dita Livraria". Translator's note.

it was trivial when compared to the vast amounts that the royal monument at Mafra and the Joanine works in Lisbon cost – the Águas Livres Aqueduct and the Patriarchal Church destroyed by the 1755 earthquake. (145) The high price of the library seems justified, when taking into account the importance of its architectural plan that guarantees it a prominent position in the history of the world's libraries. There is also the beauty of its interiors, which are amongst the most distinguished baroque examples surviving in Europe.

Despite the arrival of the books from abroad and the entry of others purchased in Portugal, the Coimbra University library, never visited by its founder king, remained closed. In 1745, the keys were given the trustee of the university, António de Sousa Azevedo, a bachelor of the university, to "take care of its cleaning and repair".[149] (146) Helped by two young men "to help putting and taking out the books and to clean the buffets and the bookshelves",[150] (147) Azevedo worked for five whole years "taking the dusty books off the shelves with the nests of swallows that entered through the windows, which were in very poor condition".[151] (148) This incredible state of negligence is repeatedly mentioned in several descriptions, albeit rare, of other 18th century Portuguese libraries. (149) At the same time, the trustee António de Azevedo made the first catalogues, according to the then existing faculties, opening "the doors of the library, with due caution, to several important people, whom he escorted and showed the contents therein".[152] (150)

---

149 In the original: "cuidar na limpeza e reparos della". Translator's note.

150 In the original: "para por e tirar os livros, e para a limpeza dos bofetes e das estantes". Translator's note.

151 In the original: "apeando das estantes todos os livros que alli se achavam em montão, cheios de muito pó, e também de ninhos de andorinhas que entravam pelas vidraças, que estavam desbaratadas". Translator's note.

152 In the original: "as portas da livraria, com a devida cautela, a muitas pessoas graves, que acompanhava e lhes mostrava o que havia naquela casa". Translator's note.

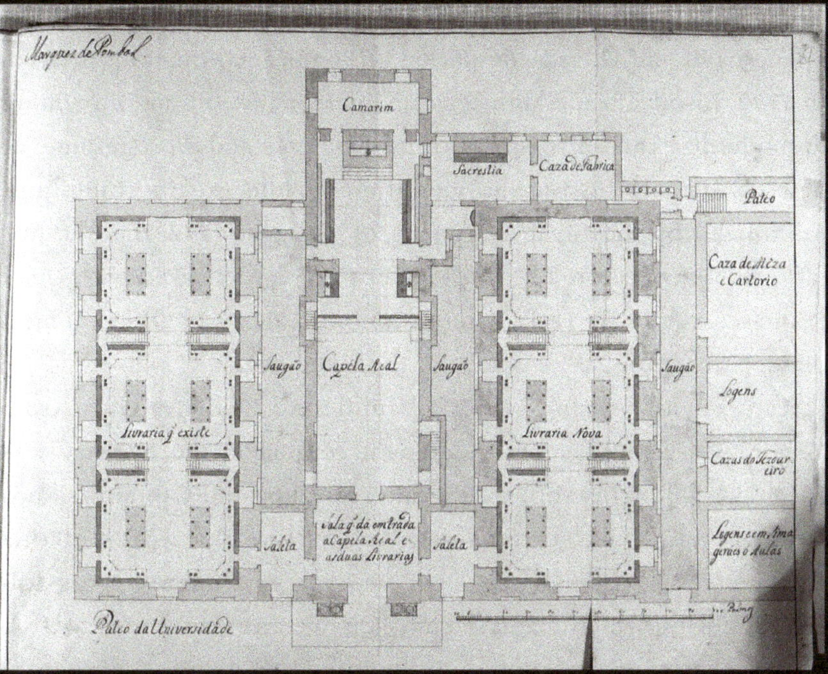

Fig. 19 Plan for the rebuilding of the Joanine Library and the Royal Chapel. CFT001.12497. Legado Robert Chester Smith, Fundação Calouste Gulbenkian, Biblioteca de Arte e Arquivos, Lisboa

Fig. 20. Drawing for the new façade of the Joanine Library and the new "Josefina" Library AUC

When the library was thus treated as a museum of curiosities, half opened and half closed, the period of Pombal reformations arrived. In 1772, José I's Prime Minister came personally to Coimbra aiming to modernize the university with new statutes and a programme of new construction work and alterations to the existing buildings. Authorized by the royal charter of 28th August 1772, the Marquis of Pombal arrived on 22nd September (151) and worked with Dean Francisco Lemos de Faria Pereira Coutinho (1770-1779) (152) until his departure on 24th October of the same year.

Later, in the spring of 1773, Guilherme Elsden arrived from Lisbon. This engineer and lieutenant colonel in the infantry was accompanied by his son, Guilherme Francisco and Captain Isidoro Paulo Pereira, also an engineer, to "outline the works of this University".[153] (153) A period of two years of intense work followed, during which magnificent plans were drawn up for a large botanical garden; the new buildings of the chemical laboratory and the academic typography; the conversion of the former Jesuit College to accommodate the natural sciences and that of the Royal College of Arts to house the university hospital. (154) Everything was done between 1773 until 1777 by a team of craftsman from Lisbon, (155) including master mason Eusébio Vicente, (156) and Master Carpenter and Woodcarver Manuel Alves Macamboa, destined to be the University master builder. (157) There were also six official artisans: the carpenter Joaquim de Carvalho, (158) the stonemasons Rodrigo de Carvalho,[154] Joaquim Inácio (159) and Dionísio Ferreira (160), the blacksmith master Pedro Pincel (161) and the sculptor António Machado. (162) Factories for roofing and other types of tile were founded, leading to large scale production, with painters

[153] In the original: "delinear as Obras desta Universidade". Translator's note.

[154] By mistake, Robert C. Smith identifies the mason Rodrigo de Carvalho as a carpenter. We have revised it to mason, the profession with which he is referred to in the original document.

such as Manuel da Costa Brioso (1719-1783) having a prominent role. (163) During these Pombal reformation years, the university rooms formed a true museum of Coimbra's rocaille style ceramic.

Within the grounds of the old university courtyard, the remarkable renovations of the 17th century *Estudos Gerais* courtyard were carried out between 1772 and 1775, under the direction of Manuel Alves Macamboa. Similar work took place on the 16th century *Paços da Universidade*, containing the large Capello room, enlarged in 1741 and which, in the following years, (164) became the Dean's residence. This building, as explained by Teófilo Braga, was "all divided with no inner communication that would serve all its parts". (165)

To correct this situation, balconies were added to the building on the exterior and interior façades, giving access to the *Gerais* courtyard and the grounds. New staircases, interior passages and a whole series of service houses were also added. (166)

During the month of his visit, the Marquis was also concerned with the other *Paço* buildings, mainly the chapel and the Joanine Library, still closed, occupying the north side of the *Gerais* courtyard. Dissatisfied with the building work, Pombal declared in an order given on 17th October 1772:

> "I have seen the improper situation of the Royal Chapel of the University and of the Library, whose smallness does not correspond to the number of books of all sciences and arts that should form the body of the Academic Library. And I have seen at the same time the above mentioned Royal Chapel, and Library with the courtyard doors, as if they were shops owned by some private citizens, exposed to the injuriousness of the weather and the inevitable indecencies of ground floor houses, the doors of which must be open in order to use them as intended. For these just and urgent reasons: I hereby declare, in the service of God and of His Majesty, that the same Royal Chapel and Library should be rebuilt

according to the plan and prospectus that were signed by me, under the inspection of the dean of the same University".[155] (167)

The plan (168) and prospectus (169) signed by Pombal show exactly what this rebuilding meant. The proposal was to tear down João III's chapel, which ran parallel to the university courtyard in the north-south direction. It would be replaced by another chapel, set on the opposite east-west axis and preceded by a monumental portal giving access to a hall or entrance room, the absence of which was noted in the order of 16th October 1772. This feature, enabling the doors to be opened to the public, at least in the physical sense, also allowed access to the library. This would be divided in two equal sections by the construction of a new building as large as the Joanine Library, which would flank the new chapel on the other side, thus doubling the space for books. The plan shows that "the existing library" and its twin "New Library" would have two small rooms on both sides communicating with the entrance room. It would also introduce, although obliquely, the protocol element of the vestibule or antechamber.

The library's imposing Joanine façade (1716-1728) would, however, be sacrificed, because the plan and prospectus offered only two rows of eight very simple windows on the main façade. In the middle of them an arch would open, flanked by two double ionic columns over high bases supporting a triangular pediment. This austere composition, by the architect Elsden, follows one of the

[155] In the original: "tendo visto a impropria situação da Real Cappella da Universidade e da Livraria della, cuja pequenez nem corresponde ao número de Livros de todas as Sciencias, e Artes, que deve formar o Corpo da Biblioteca Academica: E tendo visto ao mesmo tempo as sobreditas Capella Real, e Livraria com as portas no Patêo, como se fossem Logens de alguns Particulares, expostas às injurias do tempo, e às muitas indecências inevitáveis em cazas terrenas, cujas portas devem estar abertas para della se fazer o Uso, a que são destinadas: Com estes justos, e urgentes motivos: Hey por serviço de Deos, e de sua Magestade, que as mesmas Capella Real, e Biblioteca sejam logo reedificadas pela Planta e Prospecto della por Mim assignados, que serão com esta provisão, debaixo da Inspecção do Reytor da mesma Universidade (...)". Translator's note.

Fig. 21. Former jail in the Joanine Library.
© Sílvia Ferreira

classicizing forms of the Pombaline renovation of Lisbon's downtown architecture to the letter; and expressed in buildings like the *Arsenal da Marinha* (the naval arsenal) (170) the *Celeiro Público* (the public grain store) (171) and the original arch in *Praça do Comercio*. (172) The plans do not indicate the interior decoration, but it is logical to suppose that the magnificent woodcarving work of the Joanine building would be replaced, as in so many churches of the same period rebuilt in Pombaline times, by a banal disposition of panels combining Palladian and rococo elements, covered in paintings imitating marble in various colours. (173) The university archive actually has an undated budget for the artist António José Pinheiro to paint "various items in the library (...), book stands, shelves, balconies, etc., pearly white and imitation stone".[156] (174)

Dean Francisco de Lemos, to whom the execution of the approved plan by Pombal was entrusted, was unable to accept the idea of losing the secular chapel. He therefore decided to let time pass, without taking any definitive action: "with the mentioned works being of great expense".[157] He wrote afterwards that with

> "other buildings having greater needs, I suspended the works until this day. And looking at the best way to remedy the defects in the library house, and to expand this building without disturbing the chapel, I found that the most convenient way was that shown in the plan (...) which I made known to the Marquis Visitor, receiving no reply in this regard".[158] (175)

---

[156] In the original: "a obra da livraria (...) corpos das estantes, varandins, etc. cor de pérola e pedras fingidas". Translator's note.

[157] In the original: "Sendo as ditas Obras de grandes despezas". Translator's. note.

[158] In the original: "e havendo necessidade maior de outros Estabelecimentos, suspendi até o presente as ditas obras. E averiguando interinamente o melhor meio de remediar-se o defeito da caza da Livraria, e de ampliar-se este Edifício sem se bulir da Capella, achei que o meio mais conveniente era o que consta da planta (...) o qual fiz ver ao Marquez Visitador, e não tive resposta a este respeito". Translator's note.

Fig. 22 View of the main and south façade of the Joanine Library before the intervention of the (DGEMN) (1943-1945). CFT001.45976f. Legado Robert Chester Smith, Fundação Calouste Gulbenkian, Biblioteca de Arte e Arquivos, Lisboa

Fig. 23 View of the south façade of the Joanine Library before the intervention of DGEMN (1943-1945). CFT001.40554f. Legado Robert Chester Smith, Fundação Calouste Gulbenkian, Biblioteca de Arte e Arquivos, Lisboa

Fig. 24 Drawing of the lateral façade of the Joanine Library before the intervention of DGEMN (1943-1945). CFT001.12503. Legado Robert Chester Smith, Fundação Calouste Gulbenkian, Biblioteca de Arte e Arquivos, Lisboa

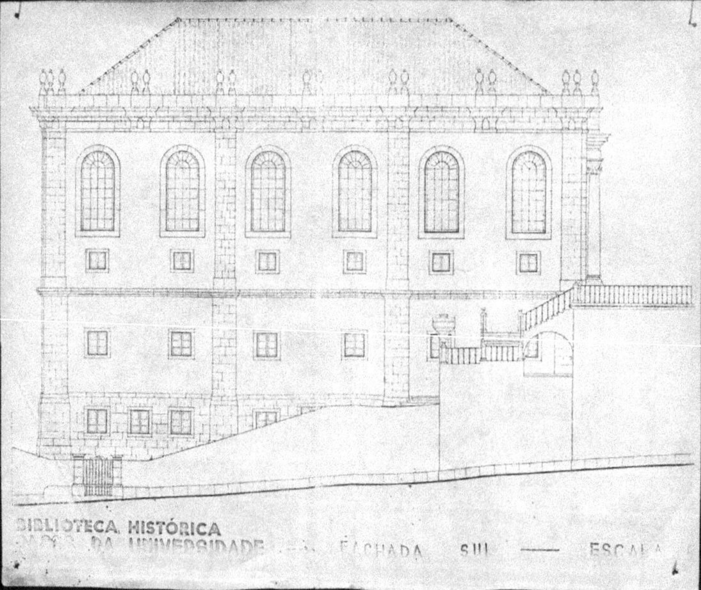

Fig. 25 Drawing of the lateral façade of the Joanine Library after the intervention of DGEMN (1943-1945). CFT001.12494. Legado Robert Chester Smith, Fundação Calouste Gulbenkian, Biblioteca de Arte e Arquivos, Lisboa

Fig. 26 The building of Joanine Library in 1974. CFT001.26486. © Robert C. Smith. Legado Robert Chester Smith, Fundação Calouste Gulbenkian, Biblioteca de Arte e Arquivos, Lisboa.

Figs. 27 e 28 The building today. © Nuno Antunes

This is how the two buildings were saved.

Having renounced the project to tear down the chapel and the Joanine Library, Dean Francisco de Lemos then proposed, on 3rd September 1773, the transfer of the university jail to "the houses that are below the current Library".[159] Approved without delay a month later, "for there is nothing more ridiculous than the vestibule of the beautiful University Hall presenting such an unworthy and sordid gaol",[160] (176) the jail was taken from the university building and installed in the basement of the Joanine Library, remaining there until 12th July 1855, when it was transferred to the former school of S. Boaventura. (177)

On 9th October 1774, the library finally opened to the public, despite its interior design not being "totally finished".[161] (178) This development was underlined by Maria I who, in 1777, nominated the first librarian, António Ribeiro dos Santos. He served until 1796, when he became the first director of the newly created Public Library of Lisbon. (179)

He was succeeded by Ricardo Raimundo Nogueira and Joaquim dos Reis, who were followed, in 1814, by António Honorato de Caria e Moura, a great mathematician, who spent 20 years in the position. (180) It was he who instituted the last important works in the library, until the disastrous 20th century "restorations".

Addressing these activities, the library historian, Florêncio Barreto Feio, listed them as "masonry and stonework, iron railings, doors, windows, bookcases, paintings and canopies".[162] (181) He goes on

---

[159] In the original: "as casas que ficam por baixo da actual Livraria". Translator's note.

[160] In the original: "por não haver coisa mais ridícula do que apresentar-se no vestibulo do bello Sallão da Universidade huma indigna e tão sordida enxovia". Translator's note.

[161] In the original: "totalmente acabado o seu arranjo interior". Translator's note.

[162] In the original: "obras de alvenaria e de cantaria, grades de ferro, portas, janellas, estantes, pinturas, e bambinelas". Translator's note.

to tell us that they continued until 18th July 1818, and "costing many thousand *cruzados*, served to conclude what was missing".[163] (182)

What were the works carried out by Dr Caria e Moura? According to Barreto Feio, one of the aims was the construction of an external passage at the level of the northern windows, connecting the library to the rest of the university complex". (183) "By a stone terrace, rather narrow but long and suitable for walking, and with iron railings on each side",[164] (184) it was possible to move directly between the library and the chapel. This kind of *galérie coursière,*[165] from which splendid views of the River Mondego and the Santa Clara area can be enjoyed, came to be considered one of the great curiosities of the library. The others, according to J. M. Teixeira de Carvalho, were the jail, the medal cabinet and the painted ceiling of the last room. (186) Also dating from these works is the current small patio, composed of six outil stone steps, commissioned from Bento Elias on 15th February 1817. (186) Within the library, there was the renovation of the twelve cabinets surrounding the three reading rooms, with new bookcases installed in each one. (187) New glass panes were put in the cabinet doors from the middle upwards, as well as "embedded doors" at the highest point of the two flanking arches, with narrow stairs leading to the galleries of the upper stands.

Whether these openings replaced previous doors or were covered for the first time, which seems unlikely, is unknown.

The windows on the west side of the library were also renovated with iron frames as protection against storms coming from the sea.

---

[163] In the original: "custando muitos mil cruzados, serviram de concluir o que faltava". Translator's note.

[164] In the original: "Por meio d´um éroximo (sic) terraço estreito, mas comprido e próprio para passeio, formado de enxelhares de cantaria, e goarnecido de grades de ferro dos lados". Translator's note.

[165] In French in the original. Translator´s note.

Barreto Feio says that the new frames replaced wooden ones, (188) which must have been introduced in the second half of the 18th century, when the old wire netting given to the library windows when it was built was discontinued. The iron frames, later applied to the six windows on the south side, as well as the railings of the external connecting passage on the other side, were executed by José Francisco Correia, "former locksmith at the university".[166] (189) Only the original iron nets on the north side of the façade remained, probably because these windows were protected by an adjacent building, now demolished.

These works from 1815-1818 made the last significant changes to the Joanine Library building before those initiated in the 1940s by the Ministry of Public Works, which so seriously defaced the monument's exterior[167]. In these arbitrary works of false restoration, as we shall see, the beautiful triglyphs and cartouches of the south façade were taken away, whose profoundly original design was so needed to dissipate the monotony inherent in the high part of the composition. This, on the other hand, was considerably increased by the introduction, on the part of the National Monument architects, using thick angular corners, pilasters, mouldings, and girdles that never existed in the building. Its southern façade was thus reduced to a brutal checkboard of smaller and larger windows, and panels[168].

---

[166] In the original: "antigo serralheiro da Universidade". Translator's note.

[167] In 1932, the Portuguese General Directorate for National Buildings and Monuments began to outline its intervention inside the library, to recover the paintings on the ceiling, a restoration that would be entrusted to the painter Joaquim Lopes in 1934. The consolidation and replacement of the ruined woodwork of the pelmets, frames and cymatiums was entrusted in the same year to the master builder, António Simões Mizarela. Cf. Raggi, G. (2018). À conquista da sabedoria: a pintura de quadratura e o programa iconográfico da Biblioteca Joanina. *Boletim da Biblioteca Geral da Universidade de Coimbra*. 48, 83-89.

[168] The documentation concerning the process of the restoration works of the 1940s in the University of Coimbra's Paço das Escolas, particulary in the Joanine Library, can be found in Direção-Geral do Património Cultural - Forte de Sacavém. *DRMC-241-266*, "Valuation of the works of the University of Coimbra Library".

The Joanine Library that, since its construction in 1716-1728, had functioned as the main library of Coimbra University, lost its distinction with the opening to the public of the new general library building, opposite the Faculty of Letters, on 29th March 1962. Since that date the library, used for special consultations has been kept intact, as the magnificent museum it is of the richest and most mature baroque phase of Portuguese civil woodwork.

Notes

1) Coimbra University, the oldest in Portugal and one of the most splendid in Europe, was actually founded in Lisbon in the late 13th century. It moved to Coimbra in 1308 but returned to Lisbon in 1338. In 1356, it moved again to Coimbra, but only for 21 years. The library stayed in the capital from 1377 to 1537, when João III installed it permanently in Coimbra. Teófilo Braga, *História da Universidade de Coimbra*, especially chapters II and III, vol. I.

(2) António José Teixeira, "Livraria da Universidade", *O Instituto*, 2nd series, vol. XXXVII, 1889-1890, pp. 305-312. online at https://digitalis-dsp.sib.uc.pt/institutocoimbra/UCBG-A-24-37a41_v037/UCBG-A-24-37a41_v037_item1/UCBG-A-24-37a41_v037.pdf.

(3) *Idem.*

(4) Bishop of Porto from 1537 to 1578.

(5) Florêncio Mago Barreto Feio, *Memória Histórica e Descriptiva à cerca da Biblioteca da Universidade de Coimbra*, Coimbra, 1857, pp. 10-11.

(6) António José Teixeira, *op. cit.*,

(7) Dean of the University from 1597 to 1605, Archbishop of Lisbon in 1627, passed away in 1630.

(8) Florêncio Mago Barreto Feio, *op. cit.*

(9) Son of the printer António de Mariz, and author of *Diálogos de Vária História em que summariamente se referem muytas cousas antíguas...com Retratos de Todos os Reis de Portugal,* Coimbra, António de Mariz, 1594 and other studies about National History. He was probably the clerk of the archive of *Torre do Tombo*, the university press agent and perpetual director of the Hospital of Vila de Castanheira. About Pedro de Mariz, see: Carvalho, J.M.T. (1914). Pedro de Mariz e a Livraria da Universidade de Coimbra. *Boletim bibliográfico da Biblioteca da Universidade de Coimbra*. 1, 389-398 and, more recently, Almeida, A.J. op. (2005) - A mobilidade do impressor quinhentista Pedro de Mariz (pp. 59-68). In Natália. M. F-A. (ed.). *Artistas e Artífices e a sua mobilidade no mundo de expressão portuguesa: actas do VII Colóquio Luso-Brasileiro de História da Arte.*

(10) Florêncio Mago Barreto Feio, *op. cit.*, p. 10.

(11) António José Teixeira, *op. cit.* The *Estatutos* of 1597 inform us that the library-keeper should be a "good Latinist" and "know Greek, and Hebrew, if possible" and have the "knowledge of the books, the know-how to order them and give an account of them". He should maintain the inventory or catalogue and provide for two reading sessions per day: one in the morning from 8 to 11, and another in the afternoon from 3 to 6. Seated in a "*cathedra* high up in said library", the library-keeper should "watch carefully over all the books, so that they are not stolen, nor badly treated". He should also demand, by a written note on the library door, that none of the "lecturers, students, or any other persons entering the said house (...) take out any book or write in them, and when they leave, close them with all the clasps the books have: and also that they do not speak to one another, in such a way as to annoy those who are studying". The respective statutes give the library-keeper the responsibility of cleaning the library and require that the Dean and principal lecturers of the faculties should visit in early August, *ibid.* pp. 307-308

(12) Archive of Coimbra University (Arquivo da Universidade de Coimbra) (AUC), *Registo das Leis, Decretos, Portarias e Mais Artigos de Legislação Relativos Á Biblioteca da Universidade,* fl. 4. Current archival reference: AUC-IV-1.ª- E-1-2-7.

(13) Dean of the University, 1639-1659.

(14) António José Teixeira, *op. cit.*

(15) AUC, *Registo das Leis (...),* fl. 4. Current archival reference: AUC-IV-1.ª- E-1-2-7.

(16) Dean of the University. 1694-1702. Born in Lisbon, he was the son of Manuel Teles da Silva, Marquis of Alegrete and of D. Luísa Coutinho. He was Dean of Lamego and Doctor of Canon Law from Braga. He passed away in 1703.

(17) Vergílio Correia, "Obras Antigas da Universidade", in *Obras,* Coimbra, vol. I, 1946, pp. 142-149.

(18) Father António Carvalho da Costa, *Corografia Portugueza e Descripçam Topografica do Famoso Reyno de Portugal,* 2nd edition, Braga, 1868-1869 vol. II, p. 15. The author praised two "notable libraries" in particular: "that of the Colleges of Our Lady of Grace, belonging to the Discalced Augustinians; and of the Society of Jesus". This quote from Robert Smith is not correct. It should read: "It has many libraries, and two of them notable, which are those of the two Colleges of Our Lady of Grace and of the Society of Jesus".

(19) *Idem, op.cit.*

(20) Son of the Marquis of Alegrete and of D. Helena of Bourbon and nephew of the canon doctor Nuno da Silva Teles, Dean in 1694-1702, *Universidade de Coimbra, Memórias da Universidade de Coimbra Ordenadas por Fr. Carneiro de Figueiroa,* Coimbra, 1937, pp. 154-155. He served in the triennium from 1715-1718 (*ibid.*, pp. 160-161). On the process of choosing a Dean, António Carvalho da Costa wrote that a Dean "is always an ecclesiastic and of great quality, approved in virtue and letters; whose period in office is triennial, according to the statute, although His Majesty usually extends it until he is provided for in some bishopric", *Corografia Portugueza e Descripçam Topografica do Famoso Reyno de Portugal,* 2nd edition, vol. II, p. 11.

(21) Declaration made on 15th January 1707.

(22) Francisco Carneiro de Figueiroa, *op. cit.*, pp. 160-161, *Registo de Leis,* fl. 4.

(23) Elmer D. Johnson, *A History of Libraires in the Western World*, New York and London 1965, p. 161. There are several reeditions of this book, the last being in 1999.

(24)[169] AUC. *Livro de Alvarás, Cartas e Provisões Régias*. Vol. 4 (1616-1746), fl. 43. Current archival reference: AUC. IV-1.ª- D-3-2-26.

(25) Dean of the University, 1719-1722.

(26) Jurist, from Porto, son of João Figueiroa Pinto, accountant of the treasury of His Majesty, and of D. Maria Carneiro de Barros. "Collegiate of St. Peter, Professor of Civil Law, Appeals Judge, Canon Doctor of Viseu, Guarda and Porto, Deputy of the Holy Office and Inquisitor in Lisbon, and Deputy of the General Council and Canon of Lisbon Cathedral. He was made Rector by His Majesty, through the Provision of 21st October 1722 and assumed his post and took the oath on 17th December of the said year". Francisco Carneiro de Figueiroa, *op. cit.*, pp. 162-165. He passed away in Porto in 1744, while still Dean of Coimbra University.

(27) Augusto Mendes Simões de Castro, *Guia Historico do Viajante em Coimbra*, Coimbra, 1880 (2nd edition), mentioned by José Ramos Bandeira, *Universidade de Coimbra*, Coimbra, 1943, vol. I, p. 140. According to Carvalho da Costa, there were 52 lecturers, *op. cit.*, vol. II, p. 9. Bernardo de Brito Botelho, writing around 1734, counted only thirty from the University and another twenty-two from the Royal College of the Society of Jesus, *Historia Breve de Coimbra*, Lisboa, 1873 (second ed.), p. 50.

(28) This contract, first published by Canon Prudêncio Quintino Garcia, in *Documentos para as Biografias dos Artistas de Coimbra*, Coimbra, 1923, pp. 352-356, was republished and reviewed by Manuel Lopes de Almeida, *Artes e Ofícios em Documentos da Universidade*, Coimbra, vol. II, 1971, pp. 294-301.

(29) The project of the grand monastery is by Fray João Turriano, from the religious order of Saint Benedict and chief engineer of Portugal; the first master builder being Domingos de Freitas. The first stone was laid on 3rd July 1649, and the nuns entered in 1677. The church, dedicated to Saint Elizabeth, was finished in 1696, Vergílio Correia and A. Nogueira Gonçalves, *Inventário Artístico de Portugal. Cidade de Coimbra*, vol. II, Lisboa, 1947, pp. 75-78.

(30) On 12th August 1721, this carpenter signed a contract to make repairs to the vicar's house in Alvorge, whose church belonged to the University, Manuel Lopes de Almeida, *op. cit.*, vol. II, pp. 368-373.

(31) [170] AUC. *Biblioteca, Livro de Registo de Receita e Despesa de Obras*, Vol. I (1717) a Vol. 11 (1728). Current archival reference: AUC-IV- 1° - E-1-2-8 a 16.

(32) [171] AUC. *Construção da Biblioteca Joanina. Férias e Materiais* (1717-1728). Current archival reference: IV- 1.ª E- 1-13 a IV- 1.ª- E-1-2-5

(33) *Idem*. 1717-1718. Current archival reference: AUC-IV-1.ª- E - 1-1-13.

(34) *Idem, ibid.*

(35) *Idem, ibid.*

(36) *Lembrança da Areia que veio de Lisboa dos gastos que fes*

---

[169] The archival reference in the original text is not correct, as it states: *Registo das Leis*. We review it.

[170] The text states: "They are in the AUC". We have entered the full archival reference.

[171] The text mentions: "Idem". We have entered the correct archival reference.

o dono da pedreira 7200

o careiro por 12 caradas 3020

os homens que arrancarão a dita areia 1200

a duas fragatas que levarão para o yate 1200

os gallegos que a tirarão da caza para as fragatas 240

duas caixas de Tintas para o emgeneiro 720

Hum Baril de pergos (sic 9420

o galego que os levou para bordo 100

despolha da areia 900

Frete para o iate .... 960"

Idem, ibid.[172]

(37) *Idem, ibid.*

(38) There were boys working for 60, 70 and 80 *réis* per day and their names are listed. *Idem. Ibid.*

(39) The numbers were between 20,000 and 50,000 men during the most intense time of the construction 1717-1730, Robert C. Smith, "The Building of Mafra", *Apollo,* April, 1973, pp. 366-367.

(40) AUC, ***Construção da Biblioteca*** *Joanina, Obras*, Cx. 1, Férias e Materiais (1717-1718).Current archival reference: AUC-IV-1.ª- E-1-1-13.

(41) "Manoel Lopes, Boatman of Carvoeira from the district of Penacova, says that he was notified by order of Your Grace to fetch some wood from Foz Dão[173] for this University and, in fact, he made two trips. And of these, he was only paid one time at 1800 and the other at 1500 *reis.* He requires the end of the payment, which is reasonable because the petitioner is a poor man and needs very much to finish being paid because the aforesaid amount is not enough for him to finish paying the men he employs on his boat". *Ibid., idem,* (April to December). Corrent archival reference: AUC-IV-1.ª E-1-1-14. Document of 18th June 1718.

(42) *Idem, ibid.*

(43) Sandelgas.

(44) AUC, ***Construção da Biblioteca***, Cx. 2 (April to December). Corrent archival reference: AUC-IV-1.ª E-1-1-14.

(45) "weekdays that begin on 29th August 1718 and end on 3rd September

Mestre Gaspar Ferreira 6 500

Caetano da Silva 5 300

Domingos Antonio 4 300

Jacinto de Araújo 6 240

Jeronimo de Moraes 3 240

João Correia ....6 ....240"

[172] It has not been possible to locate this document in the AUC.

[173] In the text: "Tobim". We have revised it to Foz Dão, as stated in the document.

Idem, ibid., Cx. 2. (April to December). Current archival reference: AUC-IV-1.ª E-1-1-14.

(46) *Idem, ibid.*, Cx. 5. (1723-1724). Current archival reference : AUC-IV-1.ª E-1-2-1.

(47) *Idem, ibid.*

(48) *Idem, ibid.*

(49) *Idem, ibid.*

(50) "On the twentieth of October of one thousand seven hundred and sixty-two, Gaspar Ferreira died with all the sacraments, a widower who survived Violante Teixeira, and had been married to Joaquina Luiza. He was buried in the Chapel of Our Lady of Conception of Saint Francis of Ponte, to where he was taken in the skiff of the Third Order and buried in the habit of Saint Francis. He was seventy-three years old and made a will in which he left his wife as executor, and I made this certificate which I signed, *era ut supra,* the priest Francisco da Cruz, AUC, parish of S. João da Cruz, *Livro de Óbitos,* 1748-96, fl. 53. Current archival reference: 1707-1795. AUC III -2.ª-E-3-5.

(51) "On the second of September of Seventeen Hundred and Twenty, I baptized Thomas, son of Bernardo Joam the students' beadle, and of his wife Maria Francisca. Thomas Antonio, student, and Violante Teixeira, wife of Gaspar Ferreira, woodcarver, were godfathers; and I signed to attest the truth of this and João da Costa Marinho of Santa Cruz represented Violante Teixeira. The priest, Antonio Gomes Carvalho, AUC *Tomo 2 dos Baptizados da Igreja do Real Mosteiro de Santa Cruz, 1626-1726,* livro 6, fl. 89. There was another Gaspar Ferreira in Coimbra at that time, collector of Santa Cruz, *Idem, ibid.*, fl. 88.

(52) Alexandre Alves, "A Santa Casa da Misericórdia de Mangualde", *Beira Alta*, vol. XVIII, 1959, pp. 29-61.

(53) Unpublished information from the District Archive of Viseu (Arquivo Distrital de Viseu) kindly given to me by Alexandre Alves.

(54) Manuel Lopes de Almeida, *op. cit.,* vol. II, p. 431. In the contract of the mason, José Rodrigues, from Alvorge, on 25th February 1722 to enlarge the residence of the vicar of this place, the "notes that were made by Master Gaspar Ferreira" are cited. *Ibid.* Vol. II, p. 375.

(55) The contract declares that Gaspar Ferreira "agreed and was contracted by this university to do the work that remains to be done in the rooms that are underneath the library of this university at a price and amount of one hundred and ninety-two thousand *reis* according to the notes that he had made for this and signed by him, and so it has been agreed to make the Tenebrae hearse, made in the form of the one in the Cathedral (...) perfect and finished at a price of nineteen thousand two hundred *reis.* And so he requested them, the Rector and deputies, to order him to do a deed of obligation for the greater security of this university and its work. By this public instrument, they have given by right the said work at the said price of one hundred and ninety-two thousand *reis* and so on plus the Tenebrae hearse at nineteen thousand two hundred". *Ibid.*, vol. III, 1974, pp. 45-47.

(56) This contract only says "the work that needs to be done on the arch of the iron gate of this university at the price and amount of one thousand *reis* according to the notes that he had made and were signed by him for that purpose". *Ibid.* vol. III, pp. 48-50. Drawn by António Tavares in Venetian style, the arch was built in the rectorate of D. Álvaro da Costa (1653-1637) by the contractor, Isidro Manuel, with the allegorical

statues being done by Manuel de Sousa, Vergílio Correia, *Obras,* vol. I, pp. 159-176, *Idem, Inventário Artístico de Portugal. Cidade de Coimbra*, Lisboa, p. 100, est. 141.

(57) On 6th March 1728, "the sum of fifty-eight thousand and four hundred *reis*" was taken from the university chest, "with fifty-two thousand *reis* being to complement the price at which the work of the arch of the railway gate of this university was tendered to Gaspar Ferreira, master of works of this university, and six thousand and four hundred *reis* for the plan that he made for the tower of the said university". AUC, *Livro de Receita e Despeza da Universidade,* vol. 1725-1728. This text was cited by J. Ramos Bandeira, *op. cit.*, vol. II, p. 6, note 3.

(58) Cf. the provision of João V, from 17th December 1728, cited *ibid.*, pp. 6-7, note 3 and by Ayres de Carvalho, *D. João V e a Arte do Seu Tempo*, Lisboa, author´s edition, vol. II, 1962, p. 363. The document states: "I make known to you, Francisco Carneiro de Figueiroa, of my council of the General of the Holy Office and Rector of the same University, that in my court of the *Meza da Consciência,* I saw your letter of twenty-fifth last October, in response to the Provision of the seventh of the said month, and year, about the works of the Tower of that University, as well as the plans you sent made by Gaspar Ferreira Master of works. (...) and by the most expert It was ordered to make the one that with this one is sent to you (with the one you sent) of the same height and grandeur, but of better manufacture, and in the form of the said new plant you will order to make the Tower, not by tender but by direct choice, giving to the said Master Gaspar Ferreira six hundred *reis* per day continuous with the proviso that he could miss only one to two days a week working on the said Tower."

(59) The attribution was made by Ayres de Carvalho, *op. cit.*, vol. II, p. 362, mainly because António Canevari (...), who spent the years 1727-1732 in Portugal, was building, in 1728, a famous clock tower in Paço da Ribeira in Lisbon, destroyed in the 1755 earthquake, *ibid.*, p. 361. Canevari's major activity in Lisbon was the beginning of the *Águas Livres* aqueduct.

(60) See note 58.

(61) The last payment was made on 27th January of that year, AUC, *Livro de Receita e Despeza da Universidade,* vol. 26, 1732-1736, fl. 74 of 1733. Current archival reference: AUC-IV-1.ª E-12-3-26.

(62) The contract was signed on 17th January 1730, M. Lopes de Almeida, *op. cit.*, vol. III, pp. 90-92.

(63) See the contract of 29th July 1729 for the work of the "altarpiece of the Main Chapel of Rabaçal Church at a price of one thousand and five *reis*, as stated in the bidding that was made for this in the form of notes and plan that Master Gaspar Ferreira" made for it. M. Lopes de Almeida, *op. cit.,* Vol. III. pp. 87-89.

(64) District Archive of Viseu (Arquivo Distrital de Viseu), *Obra da Sé,* Livro de Despezas da Mitra. Iniciado em 13 de Março of 1720.

(65) Robert C. Smith, *A Talha em Portugal,* Lisboa, 1963, p. 109 and est. 76. On Machado's woodcarving, see Flávio Gonçalves, "Uma Obra Notável de Francisco Machado", *Bracara Augusta,* vols. XXV-XXVI, 1971-1972, pp. 153-169.

(66) Robert C. Smith, *A Talha em Portugal* (...), pp. 106-108, est. 75.

(67) Robert C. Smith, *Cadeirais de Portugal*, Lisboa, 1968, pp. 61-62, est. 79. On the typed document, Smith added in pencil "The contract calling GF an 'architect resident in this same city'".

(68) *Ibid.*, pp. 58-60, est. 76 and 77.

(69) A. Alves, *op. cit.*

(70) *Ibid.*, Robert C. Smith, "Portuguese Church Tables", *The Connoisseur,* vol. CLVII, n.° 631, Set., 1964, pp. 60-65.

(71) Note on the organ? Barely legible pencil annotation by Smith.

(72) Vergílio Correia and A. Nogueira Gonçalves, *Inventário Artístico de Portugal. Cidade de Coimbra*, Lisboa, p. 75. Hellmut Wohl, "Carlos Mardel and his Lisbon architecture", *Apollo*, Abril, 1973, pp. 350-359, est. 12. See also Carlos Mardel. In *A Casa Senhorial entre Portugal, Brasil e Goa*. http://acasasenhorial.org/acs/index.php/pt/artistas/252-carlos-mardel-1695-1763.

(73) Vergílio Correia and A. Nogueira Gonçalves, *Inventário Artístico de Portugal. Cidade de Coimbra* (...), p. 75. The authors of this book attribute the gate's design to Carlos Mardel, but Wohl refutes this, believing it to be highly untypical of this architect-engineer's style, *op. cit.*, (pp. 355-356).

(74) Vergílio Correia and A. Nogueira Gonçalves, *Inventário Artístico de Portugal. Cidade de Coimbra* (...) p. 139.

(75) Esteves Pereira. Unfinished note.

(76) AUC, *Construção da Biblioteca,* Obras, Cx. 3 (1719). Current archival reference: AUC - IV- 1.ª E-1-1-15. The 1748 catalogue of the stones for the new chancel of the S. Bento da Saúde Church is comparable. The Benedictines of Lisbon bought them from around Coimbra and Tentúgal with a part of their great profits from the ships of Macao, District Archive of Braga (Arquivo Distrital de Braga), *Congregação de S. Bento*, Livro do Comercio de Macau.

(77) *Idem, ibid.* [174]

(78) *Idem, ibid.*, Cx. 4 (1720-1722). Current archive reference: AUC-IV-1.ª E-1-1-16.

(79) Contract, first revealed by Prudêncio Garcia, *op. cit.*, pp. 295-299, and republished by M. Lopes de Almeida, *op cit.*, vol. II, pp. 399-402.

(80) Prudêncio Quintino Garcia, *op. cit.*, pp. 288-294, M. Lopes de Almeida, *op. cit.*, vol. II, pp. 402-406.

(81) For the history of the payments of the three painters, based on the *Livros de Receita e Despeza of 1721-1728,* see Robert C. Smith, "O Pintor Manuel da Silva na Universidade de Coimbra", *Comércio do Porto,* 25th Sept. and 23rd Oct. 1973.

(82) Francisco Augusto Garcez Teixeira, *A Irmandade de S. Lucas*, Lisboa, 1931, p. 78.

(83) Prudêncio Quintino Garcia, *op. cit.*, p. 294. The painter João Pereira was their witness.

(84) *Ibid.*, pp. 250-253.

(85) Robert C. Smith, *Nicolau Nasoni, Arquitecto do Porto*, Lisboa, 1966, pp. 41-47 and 55-81.

---

[174] The text mentions that this document is dated from 4th November, which is not possible to check exactly on the original. Various dates appear, according to the pleading, the stated judgements, and the final decision, but because of reading difficulties, we have chosen to suppress the date in the note.

(86) Cypresses, symbolising eternity, also appear on the entrance wall tiles of the church of the former convent of the monks of St Paul in Serra de Ossa near Redondo. Dating from around 1725-1727, they are attributable to the monogram artist, P.M.P., reproduced in the article, "Convento de S. Paulo da Serra de Ossa", by Túlio Espanca, in *A Cidade de Évora*, vol. XXIX, n.º 55, 1972, pp. 149-171.

(87) As the document only says "Of making a portrait of the past Pontiff (...).7$200", Prudêncio Quintino Garcia, *op cit.*, pp. 250-253, without specifying the year of execution, may have represented the Pope Innocent XII (1691-1700) or Clement XI (1700-1721).

(88) They cost 8$000 *reis o milheiro*, importing a total of 158$424 *reis*, *Ibid.*, pp. 255-256.

(89) Agostinho Paiva, "master of white clay workshops" belonged to a large family of potters that seems to date back to the tile maker, António de Paiva, who, in 1647, laid the "carpet" tiles, purchased in Lisbon, in the university chapel, (AUC, *Capela: Documentos de obras*. Current archive reference: AUC-IV-1.ª E-2-4-20), and, a few years later, did the same service in the Great Hall of the Acts. In the Soares dos Reis National Museum in Porto, there is a blue painted plate signed "Agostinho de Paiva 1694", *ibid.*, p. XXXIII.[175] In April and September of 1701, Agostinho de Paiva received the sum of 70$000 *reis*, in payment for his *de albarrada* tiles, made for the works of the Rector D. Nuno da Silva Teles o Velho, in the *Pátio dos Gerais* and the *Casa dos Exames Privado*. Vergílio Correia, *Obras* (...), vol. I, pp. 146, 153 and 154. At the same time, he made several vases for the university chapel, which is mentioned in his petition of 1702 for the rest of his payment, AUC, *Capela: Documentos de obras*. Current archival reference: AUC-IV-1.ª E-2-4-20. The potter, João Monteiro, was paid for other vases, M. Lopes de Almeida, *op cit.* The receipts of Agostinho de Paiva for the Viseu Cathedral tiles date from 1720 and 1722, and are quoted in note 95. On 16th June 1727, the painter declared he wanted to "donate some workshops and houses that he had in the potteries that paid tribute to this Universitye" to his son Agostinho de Paiva "cleric *in menoribus*", M. Lopes de Almeida, *op. cit.* Other sons were Manuel, married to Isabel Maria Lopes on 19th October 1730, AUC, *Livro dos Cazados de S. João de Sta. Cruz*, 1711-1768, fl. 43. Current archival reference: AUC, *Paróquia de Santa Cruz de Coimbra*, C2 (1711-1768), AUC-III-2.ª D-3-4) and Mateus, who died single, aged about 51, in "Terreiro das Olarias", on 13th December 1742, *Idem*, *Livro de Óbitos de S. João de Santa Cruz*, 1707-1747, fl. 120 v.º. Current archival reference: AUC, *Paróquia de Santa Cruz de Coimbra*, O2 (1707-1795), AUC-III-2.ª D-3-5. Agostinho de Paiva died on 28th July "around ten o'clock in the evening (...) without the sacraments because they were not called in time". He was absolved "*sub condicione* and buried, on twenty-ninth of July at the Church of St Dominic as a brother in Christ", *idem*, *Ibid.*, fl. 76.

Agostinho de Paiva was first married to Antónia do Espírito Santo, the mother of his son Mateus and, secondly, to Engrácia Maria, who, widowed, married Manuel

[175] The typology of the piece is not a plate, as Robert Smith states, but a bowl. About this faience basin, signed Agostinho de Paiva and belonging to the Soares dos Reis National Museum (inv. 597Cer), see Santos, D.G. *op. cit.*, p. 221. Smith gives the date of 1694 for its creation, while Diana Gonçalves dos Santos, perhaps more cautiously, due to the difficulty of reading the complete date, does not indicate the specific year of 1690s.

da Costa Brioso, a great potter in the second half of the 18th century, son of Miguel da Costa and Maria Ferreira, *Idem, Livro de Cazados de S. João de Santa Cruz,* 1711-1768, 118 and nephew of António da Costa Brioso, potter, who died in 1740, *Idem, Livro de Óbitos de S. João de Santa Cruz,* 1707-1747, p. 106 v.°.

(90) Vergílio Correia, *Obras* (...) vol. I, est. p. 152.

(91) Today, it is the headquarters of the Santa Casa da Misericórdia de Coimbra.

(92) Today, it is the Doctor Elyseo de Moura Nursery School. http://cidemoura.pt.

(93) See (unnumbered page). These tiles are currently on the upper floor of the Cathedral cloister.

(94) By a provision of 23rd March 1724, which ordered the works' intendant, Alexandre Carneiro de Figueiredo, to pay 67$000 *reis* to Manuel da Silva, the master who painted the *grotteschi* (grotesque) tiles that came to the Cathedral, Arquivo Distrital de Viseu (Viseu District Archive), *Livro de Despezas da Mitra,* n.° 349.

(95) "I received 5 gold coins from the hand of Dr Manuel de Matos on account of the tiles I am making for Viseu Cathedral, at the price of 14$000 *reis* each thousand and, this being the truth, I asked Gaspar Ferreira to do it for me and I signed: Coimbra, today, 20th March 1720. I, Agostinho de Paiva, master potter, state that I received from the hand of Manoel da Silva, painter of the same city of Coimbra, six gold coins of 4,800 *reis*, on account of the tile that is to be made for the Viseu Cathedral, and because I am uphold the truth, and do not know how to read or write, I requested Domingos Baptista, painter, assistant in this city of Coimbra, to make this for me, and sign as witness, and his sign is that which he usually makes, today, 10th February 1722 years Agostinho de Paiva Manoel Vida." *Documentos Avulsos da Mitra de Viseu* kept in the archives of the Grão Vasco Museum in the same city.

(96) In the works of the university of 1701-1702 and Viseu Cathedral, 20 years later, the tile was laid by the same tile maker Joseph de Gois, from Coimbra. Among the documents in the Grão Vasco Museum in Viseu, there are two receipts signed by him, dated 23rd June 1720 and 25th April 1722, to the value of nine coins. Grão Vasco Museum, "Five 18th century documents concerning the tilework that covered the side walls of Viseu Cathedral and that can now be seen in the cloisters, where they were moved in 1921." Published after the death of Robert Smith by Alves. A. Artistas e Artífices nas Dioceses de Lamego e Viseu. *Revista Beira Alta.* XL, fasc 4, 456- 475, note 615 and later in the book by Santos Simões, J.M. (2010). *Azulejaria em Portugal no século XVIII.* (p. 183, note 501). (the 1979 edition updated by Maria Alexandra Gago da Câmara). Calouste Gulbenkian Foundation.

Alexandre Alves should have provided Robert Smith with these documents for the American historian to include in his study of the Joanine Library. After his death in 1975, the documentation was published by Santos Simões and Alexandre Alves himself. See Santos, D.G. *op. cit.* (p. 218).

(97) AUC, *Livro de Receita e Despeza,* vol. 23, (1721-1724), fl. 88 of 1723. The title of the document speaks of the "painting of the master niche of the casa of the d.°". Current archival reference: AUC-IV-1.ª E-12-3-23.

(98) *Idem, ibid.*, fl. 85 v.° of 1724.

(99) *Idem, ibid.*

(100) On this date, the payment of 192$000 *reis* was recalled, AUC, *Livro de Receita e Despeza da Universidade,* Vol. 23, 1721-1724, fls. 80 v.° of 1723. Current archival reference: AUC-IV-1.ª E-12-3-23

(101) The sentence comes from the contract of 28th August 1723, M. Lopes de Almeida, *op cit.*, vol. II, p. 405.

(102) See Manuel Lopes de Almeida, *op. cit.* II, p. 403: "apontamentos para o dourado e xaram da Livraria".

(103) Discharge of 40 coins given to Manuel da Silva, painter, by the Reverend Chapter, 4th August 1721: "in this city of Viseu and in the houses of Manuel da Cunha Ferreira, who was present and also Manuel da Silva, natural of the city of Lisbon and assistant in the city of Coimbra (...) the said Manuel da Silva received 40 gold coins worth 4,800 *reis* each, on account of the arrangement he had made with the Reverend Chapter of the city's Cathedral, to paint and gild the Upper Choir of the said Cathedral, and its organ". Arquivo Distrital de Viseu (Viseu District Archive), *Livro de Notas do Tabelião José Coelho de Gouveia.* The chair contains twenty-seven back panels in dark colours (green or black), with small figures and birds in gold. The organ case must have been the one, now lost, designed by Gabriel Ferreira in the same year, 1721, and carved by Manuel Correia (note 53).

(104) "Manoel da Silva, Master Painter of this city, says that he painted by order of the agent of this University, Bento Gomes Castanheira, thirty-six *varas* of flowers from the Kings' Hall and each one cost four hundred and eighty *reis* that, in all, cost seventeen thousand two hundred and eighty *reis.* He also painted the Choir of the Chapel of this University and the organ case inside and out and some large cabinets and the seats and two benches and their *genelozia.* Everything of the same choir was painted all in green, which cost twenty-one thousand six hundred *reis.* The reason for this cost being the verdigris at ten *tostois* per *aratel*[176] for the organ.

The Supplicant did the work contained in his supplication and according to his account it all cost 38$880 but supposing the verdigris was expensive, four thousand, eight hundred and eighty *reis* should be deducted, and only the rest should be paid to him, of thirty-four thousand *reis*, *V. S.ª Rm.ª* and M.es will send their own accounts to Bento Gomes Castanheira. I have received the contents from Dr Bento Gomes Castanheira, agent of the University, today 30th October 1727 Manoel da Silva", AUC, *Documentos Avulsos da Capela.* Current archival reference: AUC. *Capela: Documentos de obras*- IV-1.ª E-2-4-20.

(105) The choir of the chapel was rebuilt between 1781-1784.

(106) The news is dated 18th April, and Manuel da Silva's bid was 340$000 *reis*, Prudêncio Quintino Garcia, *op. cit.*, pp. 174-176.

(107) On 17th April, 19$200 *reis* were taken from the university chest and given to Manuel da Silva, Master Painter of this city, for the work he did in gilding the torchbearer of the paschal candle, and varnishing the Tenebrae hearse, and painting the doors of the "*açouge da feira*",[177] AUC, *Livro da Receita e Despeza da Universidade,* Vol. 24, 1724-1728, fl. 81 of 1728. Current archival reference: AUC-IV-1.ª E-12-3-24.

(108) "Manoel da Silva, Master Painter of this City, says that he gilded and painted the *back* and niche of the Sacristy of the Chapel of this University for the sum of 19$200 *reis*. 27th February 1731, *Idem, Documentos Avulsos da Capela.* Current

---

[176] See footnote 54.

[177] In the original, Slaughterhouse. Translator´s note.

archival reference: AUC. *Capela: Documentos de obras*. AUC-IV-1.ª E-2-4-20. His request of 2nd March of the same year was approved. Manuel da Silva's receipt exists in the same bundle of papers.

(109)[178] "Ferea dos ofisiais de carapinteiros que trauarão [sic] na Universidade fazendo o respaldo e o taburno para os caxois da samcristia neste anno de 1694". *Idem, ibid.*

(110) Married with Maria dos Mártires, from Penacova, had six children since 1725 to 1739, AUC, *Livro III de Baptisados da Sé, 1713-1741*, fls. 117, 166, 182 v.º., 209, 232 and 274. Current archival reference: AUC. Paróquia da Sé (Nova) de Coimbra, B3 (1713-1741). AUC-III-1.ª D-4-3.

(111) The contract to gild the altarpiece of the chancel and the images of the temple of Saint Mary of Poiares dates from 13th April 1728. M. Lopes de Almeida, *op. cit.*, vol. III, pp. 56-61.

(112) In this year, on 7th November, Gabriel Ferreira bid for the gilding of the Caria and Frexinho altars, *ibid.*, pp. 122-126.

(113) The contract speaks of "gilding and charam" for a price of 215$000, *Ibid.*, pp. 178-181. In the same year, at public auction, and along with the tile painter António Vital Rifarto, he had won the gilding of the frames of the paintings of the four Doctors of the Church, in Santa Clara, and the feinted light stone of its cross arch, all for 110$000 *reis*, Prudêncio Quintino Garcia, *op cit.*, pp. 222-224. On 21st May 1740, Gabriel Ferreira was contracted, at 369$000 *reis*, for the gilding of the main chapel of Paredes da Beira, also of the University, a work that, a year and a half later, was judged unsatisfactory, M. Lopes de Almeida, *op cit.*, vol. III, pp. 214-215 and 260-262.

(114) The contract was published by M. Lopes de Almeida, *op. cit.*, vol. II, pp. 395-398.

(115) AUC, *Construção da Biblioteca Joanina, Obras*, Cx. 5 (1723-1724). Current archive reference: AUC-IV-1.ª E-1-2-1.

(116) *Idem, Ibid.* This craftsman was one of the two guarantors of Gabriel Ferreira da Cunha, in his painting and gilding works in Caria and Freixo in 1733. M. Lopes de Almeida, *op. cit.*, vol. III, pp. 122-126. Two years later, he played the same role for António de Bastos, "*partidista*" of His Majesty's medicine, *ibid.*, vol. III, p. 135.

(117) In 1725, he was succeeded by his son, who wrote, "Albano dos Reis Salgado, official glassworker, living in this city of Coimbra, says that due to the death of his father Andre Salgado, official of the same occupation, as a glassworker of this university, the supplicant stood in his father's place, supplying the same occupation. He petitioned to this board to stay in his place and to be paid for the work of glazing that had been done as stated in the joint list. In the said glass panes was some glass that caused ugliness in the said work, and a dispatch was sent for the replacing of the glass that caused the said ugliness, and as he had satisfied everything in the form of the contract that his father made with this University". AUC, *Construção da Biblioteca Joanina, Obras*, Cx. 6 (1725-1726). Current archival reference: AUC-IV-1.ª E-1-2-2.

---

[178] In the text, the sentence is as follows: "Feria de Carpinteiros que Trabalharam na Construção do Taburno e Respaldo para os Caixoens da Sancristia, de 1694", which does not correspond exactly to the header. We have revised it to the correct version.

(118) *Idem, ibidem*

(119) *Idem, ibidem.*

(120) *Idem, ibidem.*

(121) M. Lopes de Almeida, *op. cit.*, vol. II, pp. 428-430. AUC, *Construção da Biblioteca Joanina, Obras*, Cx. 5 (1723-1724). Current archival reference: AUC-IV-1.ª E-1-2-1.

(122) AUC, *Construção da Biblioteca Joanina, Obras*, Cx. 6 (1725-1726). Current archival reference: AUC-IV-1.ª E-1-2-2.

(123) *Idem, ibidem.*

(124) *Idem, ibidem.*

(125) 12th January 1726. António Cordeiro da Geria "brought two carloads of stone from the quarry of Portunhos for the *legunja* (sic) [lisonja/work] of the Library at 400 *reis* each", *idem, ibidem.*

(126) Delivered by Manuel Francisco, *idem, ibidem.*

(127) M. Lopes de Almeida, *op. cit.*, vol. II, pp. 45-47.

(128) Florêncio Barreto Feio, *op. cit.*, p. 9. This conclusion was followed by, among other authors, the Viscount of Villa-Maior in his *Exposição Succinta da Organização Actual da Universidade de Coimbra*, Coimbra, 1877, p. 475. The building did not have an inauguration ceremony.

(129) Bernardo de Brito Botelho, *História Breve de Coimbra*, Lisboa, 1873, p. 50.

(130) AUC, *Contas de Obras da Biblioteca*, *Documentos Avulsos.*

(131) AUC, *Construção da Biblioteca Joanina, Obras*, Cx. 5 (1723-1724). Current archival reference: AUC- IV- 1.ª E-1-2-1. They were intended for the stone statue of Wisdom made by the Benedictine Fr. Cipriano da Cruz Sousa, on the side staircase to the south of the Library, Robert C. Smith, *Fr. Cipriano da Cruz, Escultor de Tibães*, Porto, 1968, p. 127 est. XXXVII. On 28th July 1691, Fr. Cipriano signed a receipt for 12$000 *reis* in payment of his image of Saint Catherine, still existing in one of the side altarpieces of the university chapel, *Idem*, Capela: *Documentos avulsos.* Current archival reference: AUC-IV-1.ª E-2-2-10.

(132) AUC, *Livro de Receita e Despeza da Universidade,* Vol. 26, (1732-1736), fl. 39 of 1733. Current archival reference: AUC-IV-1.ª E-12-3-26.

(133) AUC, *Construção da Biblioteca Joanina, Obras*, Cx. 9, (1740-1743), fl. 4 de 1742. Current archival reference: AUC-IV, 1.ª E- 1-2-5.

(134) *Idem, Obras da Biblioteca*, Cx 9. The humble phrase seems to have been a mere formality employed in the petitions. This document could not be found on the AUC.

(135) Florêncio Mago Barreto Feio, *op cit.*, pp. 42-43. La Rue (1643-1725) was the author, among other studies, of *Carmini libri IV*, Paris 1688, containing an ode in Greek on the Immaculate Conception, and four tomes of sermons (Paris, 1719), including eulogies to illustrious figures at the court of Louis XIV.

(136) 1662-1740. Ambassador of João V in London, Madrid and Paris.

(137) Unpublished research of Prof Luís Ferrand de Almeida, quoted by André Masson, *Le décor des bibliothèques*, Geneva and Paris, 1972, p. 100.

(138) Anthony Hobson, *Great Libraries*, London and New York, 1970, p. 237.

(139) AUC, *Livro de Receita e Despeza da Universidade,* Vol. 25, (1728-1732), fl. 79 v.° of 1729 and fl. 72 of 1730. Current archival reference: AUC-IV-1.ª E12-3-25. D. João da Mota e Silva (1685-1747), cardinal in 1727 and later prime minister, catalogued João V's theology books.

(140) *Idem, ibidem*. fl. 74 of 1730.

(141) Teófilo Braga, *História da Universidade de Coimbra,* 1898, vol. III, p. 268. On 24th August 1745, the amount of 1,381$456 *reis* were spent on the purchase of books in Lisbon from João Baptista Lerzo. AUC, *Livro de Receita e Despeza,* Vol. 29, (1744-1747), fl. 78 of 1745. Current archival reference: AUC- IV-1.ª E-12-3-29. Three years earlier, on 22nd May 1742, José de Sousa Baptista, agent of the university at court, gave the sum of 2,934$110 *reis* to a certain Vilas Boas[179] "for books for the library of the University and other expenses", *idem, ibidem*, Vol. 28, (1740-1743), fl. 77 v.° of 1742. Current archival reference: AUC-IV-1.ª E- 12-3-28.

(142) See the university's account books, the *Livros de Receita e Despeza*.

(143) Florêncio Mago Barreto Feio, *op. cit.*, p. 46.

(144) "Masonry and stonework: 55,915$715 *reis*; painting of the ceilings and cymatiums: 1:902$100 *reis*; painting and gilding of the bookcases, balconies, etc.: 4:245$000 *reis*; the form, woodwork and transport of the six large tables for the reading rooms: 4,410$115 *reis*; the brass signs over the main door outside and inside: 28$800 *reis*; and the portrait of Lord D. João V: 120$000 *reis*." Florêncio Mago Barreto Feio, *op. cit.*, pp. 35-36.

In 1734, the university had an annual income of 70,000 cruzados, or 1,750$000 *reis*, derived in part from its twenty-one churches, Bernardo de Brito Botelho, *op. cit.*, p. 51.

(145) Cost of the Royal Works.

(146) Florêncio Mago Barreto Feio, *op. cit.*, pp. 43-44.

(147) *Ibidem*.

(148) *Ibidem*.

(149) without reference by the author.

(150) Florêncio Mago Barreto Feio, *op. cit.*, p. 45.

(151) *Ibidem*, Augusto Mendes Simões de Castro, *Guia Histórico do Viajante em Coimbra*, 2nd edition, Coimbra, 1880, p. 174; Teófilo Braga, *Dom Francisco de Lemos e a Reforma da Universidade de Coimbra*, Lisboa, 1894; M. Lopes de Almeida. *Documentos da Reforma Pombalina*, vol. I, 1771-1782.

(152) Bishop of Coimbra, 1779-1829 and Dean for the second time, 1799-1821.

(153) There were other "helpers": Teodoro Marques Pereira da Silva, Ricardo Franco de Almeida Serra and Guilherme Elsden, of English nationality, of advanced age and suffering from gout, *ibidem*, vol. I, p. 77.

(154) A collection of these plans, mentioned in Pombal's correspondence with the Dean (M. Lopes de Almeida, vol. I, pp. 94-96 and 215) can be found in two

---

179 Smith refers to the Monsignor D. Pedro de Villas Boas Sampaio, from the Patriarchal Church of Lisbon.

folders entitled *Provisões do Marques de Pombal* and *Plantas Referentes às Obras Projectadas por Ocasião da Reforma da Universidade de Coimbra, in 1772*, nºs. 3083 and 3084 in the Manuscript Section of the General Library of Coimbra University.

(155) M. Lopes de Almeida, *Documentos da Reforma Pombalina*, vol. I, p. 99.

(156) "Distinguished Master Mason, and a good fortifier of the Works he executes", *ibidem*, p. 96. "He received, as a salary, 600 *reis* per day", *ibidem*, p. 99.

(157) He was the true successor of Gaspar Ferreira, who died in 1762, in the variety and distinction of his activities. He came from Lisbon, in 1774, as he himself indicates, in an extraordinary document from the AUC, of 1796, in which he requested an increase of his daily 600 *reis*, for having assumed the functions of master of masonry and stonework and also of architect, "doing as he has done, since the absence of the Engineers, all the drawings, and necessary designs, not only of the University works but also of the Royal Convent of Santa Clara". AUC. *Universidade, Documentos de Despesas de Obras*, Cx. 3. Current archival reference: AUC- IV-1.ª E-10-1-3. He worked there as a carver, like Gaspar Ferreira, in this capacity, he designed, in 1783 or 1784, the new altarpiece for the main chapel of Our Lady of the Assumption of Dine (Bragança), belonging to the University, Current archival reference: AUC. *Documentos relativos a bens no bispado de Bragança* (Col). IV-1.ª E-22-3-2. As master carpenter, he designed a windbreaker for the university chapel, which does not exist anymore (Undated notes in the AUC). As an architect, Manuel Alves Macamboa drew up the plans for the university's astronomical observatory, built in 1790-1799 and demolished years ago.[180] Futhermore, according to data provided in 1974 by the parish priest, he designed the S. Bartolomeu Church façade, in Coimbra, a building begun in 1756.[181] He also designed the majestic Santa Casa da Misericórdia Hospital, in Viseu. As a contractor and master builder of the university, he directed the construction of the Chemical Laboratory, designed by Elsden (1775-1776, AUC, *Livro das Folhas de Despeza*, fl. 1 v.º) and several other buildings, as well as the renovation of the *Patio dos Gerais* (1779). In 1781, he inspected the renovation of the university chapel, *idem, Documentos Avulsos da Capela*. He was still acting as master builder in 1807, when, in May of that year, he visited the S. Miguel de Passos University Church, and prepared "plans, prospectus and section" of it and notes for its renovation, *idem*. In 1793, Manuel Alves Macamboa drew up the plans for the transparent lighting in the university portal and courtyard, featuring the figure of Abundance, *Idem, Contabilidade e Administração das Obras*. Current archival reference: *Livro do Registo de Receita e Despesa das Obras*, 1775-1776. AUC-IV-1.ª E-10-2-31.

(158) *Idem, Livro das Folhas de Despeza*, 1773, fl. 9 v.º.

(159) *Idem, ibidem*, fl. 1.v.º.

(160) In 1775, he worked in the university halls, *idem, ibidem*, fl. 17.

(161) *Idem, ibidem*, fl. 25 v.º.

(162) *Idem, ibidem*, fl. 28 v.º. The payment to António Machado, sculptor, was made on September 7th 1776.

---

180 Correia, V., Gonçalves, A. *op. cit.* (p. 107).

181 *Idem*. (p. 39).

(163) A. A. Gonçalves, "Breve Noção sobre a História das Ceramicas em Coimbra", in Charles Le Pierre, *Estudo Chimico e Technologico sobre a Ceramica Portugueza Moderna*, Lisboa, 1899, p. 237.

(164) AUC, *Livro da Receita e Despeza da Universidade,* Vol. 28, 1740-1743, fl. 80 (1741). Current archival reference: AUC-1.ª E-12-3-28 and Vol. 32 (1756-1759), fl. 78 v.º (1758). Current archive reference: AUC-IV-1.ª E-12-3-32.

(165) Teófilo Braga, *D. Francisco de Lemos e a Reforma da Universidade de Coimbra* (...), pp. 78-79.

(166) *Ibidem*, p. 122.

(167) Biblioteca Geral da Universidade de Coimbra, *Manuscritos*, cód. 3083, fl. 62.

(168) *Idem, ibid.* Pink, grey and yellow wash pen-and-ink drawing signed by the Marquis of Pombal. It measures 34.5 cm x 44 cm.

(169) *Idem, Ibidem.* Pink, grey and yellow wash pen-and-ink drawing signed by the Marquis of Pombal. It measures 27 cm. x 61.5 cm.

(170) Drawn by Eugénio dos Santos e Carvalho (1711-1760) and built in 1759.

(171) Rebuilt by the drawings of Eugénio dos Santos e Carvalho between 1765 and 1768.

(172) José Augusto França, *Une ville de lumiere, la Lisbonne de Pombal*, Paris, 1965, p. 100, est. XXV.

(173) Robert. C. Smith, *The Art of Portugal (1500-1800),* Lisboa, 1968, est. 76.

(174) It was not possible to locate in the AUC the document referred in the text.

(175) Teófilo Braga, *História da Universidade de Coimbra,* vol. III, p. 507.

(176) M. Lopes de Almeida, *Documentos da Reforma Pombalina*, vol. I, p. 103.

(177) José Ramos Bandeira, *op. cit.,* vol. I, 1943, p. 146.

(178) *Ibidem,* pp. 146-147.

(179) Florêncio Mago Barreto Feio, *op. cit.*, pp. 46-47, 56-57 and 65.

(180) *Ibidem,* pp. 67, 69 and 71.

(181) *Ibidem*, p. 73.

(182) *Ibidem.*

(183) *Ibidem*, pp. 75-76.

(184) *Bric-à Brac. Notas Históricas e Arqueológicas,* Porto, 1926, p. 398.

(185) *Ibidem.*

(186) AUC, *Livro de Registo de Folhas Correntes de Obras,* Vol. 3, (1816-1818), fl. 88. Current archival reference: AUC-IV-1.ª E-10-2-21.

(187) Florêncio Mago Barreto Feio, *op. cit.*, pp. 75-76.

(188) *Ibidem.*

(189) *Ibidem.*

II – ARCHITECTURE AND ART

On the 15th of January, 1707, John V of Portugal, in a solemn ceremony held a few months after his accession to the throne declared himself “Protector of the University of Coimbra”. (1) It was not, however, until almost a decade had elapsed that the new king was to make the magnificent gift which so closely associates him with the University. The kingdom was engaged in the difficult and uncertain negotiations to end the War of the Spanish Succession, in which Portugal had undertaken costly and futile campaigns of support of the unsuccessful candidate, the Archduke Charles of Austria. After the signing of the peace at Utrecht in February of 1716, as a Portuguese art historian of the late XVIII century has remarked, “the realm began to recuperate and John the Fifth could turn his attention to science and the fine arts”. (2)

For this he found and ideal expression in the decision to present a new library to the University of Coimbra (3). A royal provision of October 31,1716 makes known that His Majesty granted permission to erect a building for the library facing the courtyard of the university on whatever site would be most useful and least expensive and approves the purchase by the university of the library of Francisco Barreto for the price of fourteen thousand *cruzados*. (4)

For the new library a location was chosen at the southwest corner of the court, adjacent to the Manueline chapel and commanding a fine view down the valley of the Mondego to the hills of the Beira Baixa beyond. Work began at once and was officially concluded

Fig. 29 Aerial view of the Paço das Escolas with the Mondego in the background. © Nuno Antunes

Fig. 30 Aerial view of the Paço das Escolas with the Joanine Library on the left. © Nuno Antunes

eleven years later, in 1728 (5), although some of the details of the decoration still remained to be completed as late as 1733. (6)

The Royal Library at Coimbra is one of John V´s two most important undertakings in architecture that have survived, the other being the royal convent and palace of Mafra, which begun in 1717, on plans of João Frederico Ludovice. A third great monument, the patriarchal church in Lisbon, was destroyed completely in the earthquake of 1755. (7) The library symbolizes a real love of learning on the part of the monarch, which in 1721 led him to found the Portuguese Academy of History and to support it actively throughout his lifetime. The royal library is also one of the most beautiful buildings erected in Europe during the first half of the eighteenth century. For these reasons it is especially unfortunate that the name of its architect is not known.

In the archive of the University of Coimbra the accounts for the building are on file. Although they are voluminous and provide a great deal of information as to payments to minor executants, (8) nowhere is there any indication as to who was responsible for the plan and decoration of the structure. The contract, if there was one, may have remained at the court in Lisbon and could well have perished with so many other documents in the earthquake of 1755. It has been suggested that Ludovice as royal architect may have given the design. (9) Against this surmise, however, is the fact that he is not known to have entered the king´s service until 1717 and the more important circumstances that nothing about the library of Coimbra shows any close relation to Ludovice´s work, which was always predominantly Italianate with a few occasional reflections of the taste of his German homeland. (10) On the other hand, the building is full of connections with Claude de Laprade. Consideration of this connections leads inevitably to the conclusion that the French sculptor must have played the major role in the decoration of the building.

As we have seen, Laprade had worked extensively and apparently with success for the University of Coimbra.[182] In this respect it should be noted that among the commissions he had carried out for D. Nuno da Silva Teles had been the decoration of the door of what was then the library of the University with an appropriate relief representing books. (11) The marble Portrait of John V in the sacristy of S. Vicente at Lisbon, (12) had probably brought him into contact with the donor of the new library building[183]. These accomplishments alone could have recommended Laprade for consideration in connection with this structure. To them can also be added the novelty of his style, which was based in such large measure on the style of Louis XIV, a sovereign whose magnificence John V so much admired that he was with difficulty restrained from going with a great retinue to visit Paris and Versailles, once the peace of Utrech had been signed. (13) To have a great French library at Coimbra and a fine Italian church and residence at Mafra may have seemed a fair substitute to the king thwarted in his plan to travel. This again, however, is mere hypothesis. Yet even if one cannot accept the possibility that a relatively little-known French sculptor working in the provinces could have received so great commission, internal evidence indicates that whatever design for the library may have been sent in from outside Coimbra was greatly modified by Claude de Laprade.

The building consists of one principal storey covering an area approximately 35,5 m x 17,5 m. The entrance front, which faces the courtyard, is dominated by a great portal of local stone above

---

[182] Smith, R. C. (1954). Early works of Claude Laprade and the style Louis XIV in Portugal. *Gazette des Beaux-Arts*. October, 163-190.

[183] The marble portrait of king John V in the sacristy of the monastery of São Vicente de Fora, in Lisbon, is attributed by Smith to Laprade without documental evidence. On this subject see the book chapter of Saldanha S.C. (2010) - A escultura em São Vicente de Fora: projecto, campanhas e autores (pp. 195-196). In Sandra C. S. (ed.). *Mosteiro de São Vicente de Fora. Arte e História*. Centro Cultural do Patriarcado de Lisboa, where this author refutes this attribution.

a broad low *perron*[184] of five almost imperceptibly rising steps. These two stone elements, beautifully proportioned in relation to the full façade, contrast their golden colour with the whitewashed surfaces of the walls. The design of the portal, which consists in essence of a handsome arch between paired Ionic columns carrying a section of entablature, is reminiscent of J.H. Mansard´s façades at Versailles and the Grand Trianon and is also closely related to a triumphal archway designed by Daniel Marot, the *émigré*[185] French architect and decorator a decade or more before. (14) The panelling of the stone reveals behind the columns with circular disks between rectangular compartments a further link with the art of Louis XIV, for this was a device frequently employed at Versailles.

To these general French qualities must be added the catalogue of the personal mannerisms of Claude de Laprade that can be found upon the entrance façade of the library. One of the most striking of these is the series of seven decorated bosses in the form of birds and rosettes that project from the soffit of the arch in exactly the same fashion as those in the hood of the monument of Joseph I[186] nearby and which are also related to the funeral sculptures of the arch of the tomb at Vista Alegre.[187] (15) The arch of the library

---

[184] Originally in French, staircase.

[185] Originally in French, emigrant.

[186] The effigy of D. José I is nowadays integrated in the portal of the *Gerais*. The portal was commissioned during the rectorate of D. Nuno da Silva Teles to Claude Laprade. The initial bust was supposed to be that of D. Pedro II, later replaced by the one of D. José I at the time of the reform of the *Gerais*, under the supervision of the Marquis of Pombal. Cf. Pimentel, A.F. (2000) - Cidade do saber/ cidade do poder: a arquitectura da reforma (pp. 265-268). In Ana A. (ed.). *O Marquês de Pombal e a Universidade*. Imprensa da Universidade de Coimbra; *idem*, (2011) - A Biblioteca da Universidade e os seus espaços (pp. 11-21). In A.E. Maia do Amaral. (ed.). *Tesouros da Biblioteca Geral da Universidade de Coimbra*. Imprensa da Universidade de Coimbra, and Mendes, P. e Fiolhais C. (2013) - *Biblioteca Joanina, Universidade de Coimbra*. (pp. 25-26). Imprensa da Universidade de Coimbra.

[187] It refers to the tomb of the bishop of Bragança-Miranda, D. Manuel de Moura Manuel, sculpted by Laprade in 1689 and commissioned by the same bishop, situated in the chapel of Our Lady of Penha at the Quinta da Vista Alegre in Ílhavo,

Fig. 31 Façade of the Joanine Library. © Nuno Antunes

Fig. 32 View of the Grand Trianon. Versalhes. France. © Maria João Petisca

Fig. 33 Intradorse from the Joanine Library portal.
© Sílvia Ferreira

Fig. 34 Intradorse from the Pórtico dos Gerais. Universidade de Coimbra. Portugal © Sílvia Ferreira

Fig. 35 Intradorse from the arch of the funerary monument of D. Manuel de Moura Manuel. Chapel of Vista Alegre, Ílhavo, Portugal © Sílvia Ferreira

doorway springs from impost blocks carried on long brackets to which are affixed birds quite similar to their treatment to the phoenix and eagle of the monument of bishop of Miranda. The columns have more evidence of Laprade´s hand to disclose, for in the capitals, whose volutes seem large in scale for the shafts, are set diminutive masks almost exactly like those at Vista Alegre and in the costumes of the statues for the classrooms of the University of Coimbra.[188] (13) Here they may represent some reminiscence of the heads of Apollo used in the same position in the capitals of the so-called French order that Charles Lebrun designed for the Louvre or other variants on this same theme. (17) These masks reappear on the waterspouts in the cornice of the library building, following a custom which had lapsed since Manueline times. To revive it is characteristic of Laprade, for it fitted in with his own piquant tastes in decoration, which the ornamental bosses of late Gothic Portuguese vaulting had already found favour. Addition of evidence of a respect for the practices of the country is found in the use of broad pilaster strips of masonry at the angles of the building, which along with the simplified cornice and parapet frame sparkling whitewashed walls. This is a capital characteristic of all Portuguese building of the late XVII and early XVIII centuries. (18)

At this point it is appropriate to note that a design similar to that of the façade of the Library at Coimbra had already appeared in Lisbon. It is seen on one of the arches erected at the time of the marriage of John V in 1708. This arch had a central opening

---

northern Portugal. Cf. Ferreira, S. (2017) - From Stone to Wood: Claude Laprade (c.1675-1738) and his Journey from Provence to Portugal (pp. 53-59). in Kathrin W., Jessica D., Matej K. (eds.). *Artists and Migration 1400-1850. Britain, Europe and beyond*. Cambridge Scholars Publishing; *Idem* (2019) - Claude Laprade: um escultor do Barroco entre a Provença e Portugal (pp. 174-183). In Paulo A. F., Ana Paula A. (eds.). *Lisboa Plural: 1147-1910*. Museu de Lisboa.

[188] It refers to the statues that Laprade sculpted for use in the university classrooms. They include those of Justice, Medicine, Geography, etc.

Fig. 36 Bird in the decoration of the portal arch of the Joanine Library.

Fig. 37 Detail of the Bishop of Miranda´s tomb. Chapel of Vista Alegre. Ílhavo. © Sílvia Ferreira

Fig. 38 Capitals and volutes with masks. Portal of the Joanine Library of Coimbra. CFT001.12365 © Robert C. Smith. Legado Robert Chester Smith Fundação Calouste Gulbenkian, Biblioteca de Arte e Arquivos, Lisboa.

Fig. 39 Detail of the coat of arms of Bishop Manuel de Moura Manuel with mask at the bottom. Capela da Vista Alegre. Ílhavo. © Sílvia Ferreira

Fig. 40 Spout on the cornice of the Joanine Library. © Nuno Antunes

framed by a paired Ionic pilasters surmounted by herms with raised arms. There was a cushion frieze in the entablature and an oval targe over the center of the cornice.[189] These details all suggest the authorship of Claude de Laprade. (19)

Finally, there is evidence contained in a latin inscription inside the library building. Upon a scroll accompanying a female figure identified as *Universitas*, which is part of the painted ceiling of the center room of the library, are the words:

> "CLAUDITE JAM RIVOS PUERI SAT.
> PRATA BIBERUNT"

This quotation, which is the last line of Virgil´s third eclogue, can be translated "Close, oh, boys, the streams, the banks have drunk their fill.[190] (20) Its significance lies not in the meaning of these words but in their position. The hexameter has been deliberately broken so as to create two lines instead of one and thus bring the two words *Claudite* and *Prata* together. Certainly, these two Latin words suggest the name of Claude de Laprade.

There can be no doubt that the inscription was chosen because it presented an allusion to the name of the French sculptor and this is emphasized by the deliberate breaking of the line. One can think of no reason why the sculptor´s name should have been evoked in this typically donnish fashion upon the walls of the library of

---

[189] Robert Smith referes to the arch of the English described in (1708). *Discripçam do arco triunfal que a naçam Ingleza mandou levantar (...).* (p. 4). Officina de Valentim da Costa Deslandes. This arch was designed by the maltese artist Gimac and not by Claude Laprade, as this text proves. About the life and works of Gimac see: Carvalho A. (1962) - *D. João V e a arte do seu tempo.* (pp. 246-311). Author´s edition. We think that what Smith might mean in this passage is that Laprade probably collaborated in the design and execution of some of the arches for the wedding celebrations of King John V., sculpting some of its statues.

[190] Free translation by Robert C. Smith.

the University of Coimbra unless he had something to do with its creation. For these various reasons, therefore, it seems permissible to attribute to Claude de Laprade a major role in the planning and decorations of the royal library of Coimbra.

The *mise-en-scène* of the façade is sober, almost austere, in comparison with the earlier works of the sculptor. But here, it must be remembered, Laprade was dealing with architecture and not sculpture and this simplicity was a part of the immediate architectural tradition of both France and Portugal. Also, it is possible that a more mature Laprade had now realized the value of restraint in carefully coordinated exterior decoration. That is proved in this instance by the effectiveness of the superb targe with the royal arms and the crown, a grand plastic composition which dominates the plain, flat, ordered ensemble around it. Here again can be discovered the hand and spirit of Laprade. This time there are seen in the groaning mask at the base and the ruffled shell, from which water seems to pour, at the top, in the flowers and birds of the great pendent garland and also in the curious, richly ornamented reed-like devices on both sides of the shield. The inner ones have a baroque spiral form that considerably animates the sense of movement throughout the targe. The outer ones terminate in small balls that establish a sensitive relation with the lids of the curiously shaped urns of the parapet and also provide a point of contact with the woodwork of the library´s interior. Entries in the University´s book of accounts for payments to individuals in the course of the work establish the approximate date of the doorway. In the month of December, 1719, payment was made for a machine to lift and set in place the columns and lintel of the "pórtico da Livraria".[191] By April of 1720 the work had been completed. (21)

[191] In Portuguese, Portal of the Library.

Fig. 41 Ceiling of the central room of Coimbra's Joanine Library. CFT001.02897 © Robert C. Smith. Legado Robert Chester Smith, Fundação Calouste Gulbenkian, Biblioteca de Arte e Arquivos, Lisboa.

Fig. 42 Ceiling of the central room of Coimbra's Joanine Library. © Nuno Antunes

HANC AVGVSTA DEDIT LIBRIS COLLIMBRIA SEDEM,
VT CAPVT EXORNET BIBLIOTHECA SVVM.

The three fine rooms, each measuring approximately 9,5m. x 13m., of this *"magnifico edifício"*[192] have since their completion been widely and justly admired. (22) On occasions they have been compared with the interior of Johann Fischer von Erlach´s Imperial Library, in Vienna, which dates from 1721. (23) The comparison, however, is, unwise, for the two buildings have little in common beyond the allegorical paintings of their ceilings and the sumptuous display of their books. The Austrian library is an Italianate structure whose interior relies for its effect upon a sense of vast internal space induced by a single enormous room lighted by a cupola and framed in walls of stone. At Coimbra the space of the interior is deliberately subdivided in such a way as to produce three almost identical unvaulted interiors, the proportions of which are small enough to keep the walls close to the spectator. This is essential to the success of the decoration, which in spite of its grandiose pattern has a kind of intimacy produced by the warmth and small-scale complications of the gilded and polychromed carved wood of which it is almost entirely composed.

In both respects the interior is eminently Portuguese. In Portugal mere bigness has practically always been rejected in favour of constructions of moderate proportions which are frequently unvaulted. The woodcarved interior, one of the greatest accomplishments of Portuguese art, was in the early XVIII century attaining the summit of its splendour. (24) Whoever, therefore, designed the interior of the Library at Coimbra was thoroughly familiar with Portuguese taste, as Claude de Laprade would have been after a residence of two decades in that country, at the very beginning of which he had started to introduce Portuguese elements into his work. In the woodcarving some of the motifs of the façade are repeated and there are others which inevitably lead the spectator back to earlier works

[192] In Portuguese, outstanding building.

by Laprade. As a result, the interior of the library, as the Virgilian inscription implies, is dominated by his personality. To him must we ascribed the principal features of the decoration, although to argue that himself, hitherto only a sculptor of stone, executed any large part of the woodcarving would be unjustified either by the weight of internal evidence or the authority of know documentation. Only occasionally does the woodwork suggest the personal mannerisms of Laprade. There can be no doubt that most of it was carved by a group of craftsmen directed by the *mestre entalhador,*[193] or master woodcarver, João Roiz de Almeida, for the names of some of them are preserved in the account for the work in the University Archives. (25)

The interior of the Library at Coimbra is like the prolongation of its exterior, so great is the sense of unity that the building conveys. The great arched portal that dominates the façade is repeated four times inside the library, the wooden surfaces being painted with rose and cream-colored veins to simulate marble. The treatment of these arches is basically the same as the one on the exterior. Here are the same brackets with birds, single on the entrance and terminal walls of the building, doubled on the arches with two faces attached to the partitions dividing the rooms. Here are the same bosses on the soffits of the arches, although these are now gilded, like the brackets below them, and the alternating pendants, which are somewhat increased in length. Above the arches are placed targes capped by the royal crown with lateral devices of eccentric formation closely resembling the elements around the shield on the exterior. Enormous, gilded garlands identical with that of the façade, except for the small birds which here are mitted, fall from the targe and are fixed in swags to the wall with large golden rings. The targes themselves are decorated with symbols of the faculties of the university quite in the spirit of Laprade reliefs for the over-

[193] In Portuguese, "master woodcarver".

Fig. 44 View of the rooms of the Joanine Library. © Nuno Antunes

Fig. 45 Cartouches surmounting the arches that divide the rooms of the Joanine Library. © Nuno Antunes

doors of the *Pátio dos Gerais.*[194] One in particular representing a number of books upon a draped table, is practically identical. (26)

The great polychromed shield with the royal arms, which is set above the Portrait of the Donor (27), at the end of the third room, includes in its rich border the motif of a gaping mask framed by a shell. This is a device which, though by no means an invention of the sculptor, is intimately associated with his work. So also are the long faces, pouting mouths and rubbery arms of the flying putti attached to the upper part of the shield, details which may have been personally carved by Laprade, and the precise iconography of the banners that hang from the trumpets of the angels below them. One of these displays the royal armillary sphere and the cross of the military Order of Christ, while the other presents a rotund owl as a symbol of library knowledge. (28)

The double brackets of the cornices, to which small, tight garlands are attached, recall the monument of Joseph I as do also the baskets of flowers and the tapering bases and balusters of the balconies around the bookcases (fig.5). These *gaines,*[195] so popular with the furniture designers of Louis XIV, are almost identical in their shape and floral decoration with the bases of the half-length Atlantids of the old portal of the *Gerais* and thus supply more evidence for the argument to prove Claude de Laprade´s connection with the library. These unusual supports terminate at the top in volute-like corkscrew forms that recall the kind of velvet ornaments used by Marot and other French designers for state beds and other ceremonial furniture. Much of the woodwork of the three rooms is skilfully ornamented with red and dark chinoiserie decoration (fig. 6). The pseudo-oriental paintings are themselves strongly suggestive of French influence and specifically that of the period of Louis XIV, when all-over decoration

---

194 In Portuguese, courtyard of the "Gerais".

195 In French in the original.

Fig. 46 Overlapping cartouche in a door at the *Pátio das Aulas dos Gerais.* University of Coimbra. © Nuno Antunes

Fig. 47 Birds in the arches that divide the rooms of the Joanine. © Nuno Antunes

Fig. 48 Decorative composition above the portrait of the King John V. CFT001.12415 © Robert C. Smith. Legado Robert Chester Smith, Funda-

Fig. 49 Detail of the balustrades of the balconies of the Joanine Library with flower baskets. CFT001.12326 © Robert C. Smith. Legado Robert Chester Smith, Fundação Calouste Gulbenkian, Biblioteca de Arte e Arquivos, Lisboa.

Fig. 50 Third room of the Joanine Library with the portrait of the king John V. © Nuno Antunes

Fig. 51 Estipies of the Joanine Library. CFT001.27228

Fig. 52 Detail of the chinoiserie painting in the Joanine Library. CFT001.12319 © Robert C. Smith. Legado Robert Chester Smith, Fundação Calouste Gulbenkian, Biblioteca de Arte e Arquivos, Lisboa.

of this sort, which appears in one of the most famous Marot´s interior designs, enjoyed a special popularity. (29)

One major reflection of the interior of the library exists in Coimbra. This is the small sacristy of the little pilgrimage church of *Sto. António dos Olivais*, which cannot be dated more precisely than the first quarter of the XVIII century. (30) The principal connections of this beautiful small apartment with the library are the wooden arch of the altar niche with abbreviated boss decorations in the soffit, the ruffled shells of the pediment and the keystone and the carving of the pilaster strips which recall the "capitals" of the bookshelves (fig. 7). In the broad gilded band that passes around the center of the walls, incorporating garland-spouting masks (31) under canopies like the peeled skins of bananas, there are other reminders of Laprade. These do not seem strong enough, however, to authorize attribution of the sacristy to the sculptor. It seems wiser to consider it the work of someone deeply impressed with his manner, one or more perhaps of the sculptores who had worked at the Library of the University of Coimbra. (32)

There is in Aveiro, on the other hand, a building of the period which seems undoubtedly to show the direct intervention of Claude Laprade. The church of the Senhor Bom Jesus das Barrocas was begun in 1707 for an *Irmandade*,[196] or lay brotherhood, of fisherman (33), who like those of Matosinhos near Oporto, attributed unusual powers to an image of Christ crucified, in their possession. (34) The church was completed in 1722 (35), on an octagonal plan, which, according to Dr. Reynaldo dos Santos, suggests the hand of the royal architect João Antunes (36), who was at Aveiro early in the XVIII century in connection with the tomb of the Infanta Santa, at the convent of Jesus, and who was fond of this kind of polygonal building. The attribution is convincing, because of the austere Mannerist style of the granite structure and its resemblance to a known work

[196] In Portuguese.

Fig. 53 Sacristy of the church of Saint Anthony of Olivais. Coimbra.
© Sílvia Ferreira

Fig. 54 Triumphal arch of the sacristy chapel of the church of Saint Anthony of Olivais. Coimbra. © Sílvia Ferreira

Fig. 55 Altar of the sacristy chapel of the church of Saint Anthony of Olivais, Coimbra. © Sílvia Ferreira

Fig. 56 Mask above the chests of the sacristy of the church of Saint Anthony of Olivais Coimbra. © Sílvia Ferreira

of Antunes, his church of the Senhora da Cruz at Barcelos, and the design attributed to him of the church of the Menino Deus in Lisbon. (37) The octagonal plan of the latter, repeated at Barrocas, was varied in a number of chapels built at Aveiro in the early XVIII century, the largest of which is the hexagonal one of S. Gonçalo, dated 1714 by an inscription over the door.[197] Unlike these lesser buildings, however, the church of the Senhor das Barrocas was decorated, at least on the exterior, with what approaches a royal magnificence.

This is expressed in the form of three portals of *Ancã* limestone, which have unfortunately suffered considerable damage from exposure to strong winds sweeping in from the sea and from a long period of neglect, during which the *Irmandade*[198] seems almost to have abandoned its handsome edifice. The design of the three portals shows unmistakable evidence of the style of Claude de Laprade (38), but this time with the addition of new significant elements. (fig. 8 and 9)

In the side doors the decoration consists of a richly framed targe displaying a mutilated emblem set between genii who sprawl on the pediment and a pair of acanthus "brackets" joining the severe frame of the door to the projecting frieze above it. (fig.8 pormenor?)

Alberto Souto has properly called attention to the analogy of the whole upper area with the over-doors of the University of Coimbra[199], where the practically identical relief of a draped table was used (39), but he does not mention the equally arresting connections with the decoration of the University library.

This begins with the reliefs of draped tables over the interior arches. It continues with the acanthus brackets, which occupy exactly the same position in regard to the architectural members and have

[197] See the recente study of Pimentel. H. (2018). *Plantas Centralizadas na Cidade de Aveiro: A capela do Senhor das Barrocas (1722-1732)*. (Master dissertation in Architecture, FCTUC).

[198] In Portuguese, Brotherhood.

[199] Smith refers to the emblems on the upper doors of the classrooms of the *Gerais*.

Fig. 57 Portal of the church of Our Lord of Barrocas before 1959, with the two adult angels above the entablature. Postcard. Provided by José Rebocho Cristo

Fig. 58 Portal of the church of Our Lord of Barrocas after 1959. One of
ne angels had already fallen. In Nogueira Gonçalves, A (1959) - Inventário
Artístico de Portugal. Distrito de Aveiro. VI. Lisboa

Fig. 59 Façade of the church of Our Lord of Barrocas. Aveiro.

Fig. 60 Church of Our Lord of Barrocas. Main Portal. Aveiro.
© Sílvia Ferreira

Fig. 61 Church of Our Lord of Barrocas. Detail of the main portal. © Sílvia Ferreira

Fig. 62 Church of Our Lord of Barrocas. Detail of the intradorse of the main portal arche. Aveiro. © Sílvia Ferreira

Fig. 63 Church of Our Lord of Barrocas. Side door. Aveiro.
© Sílvia Ferreira

Fig. 64 Church of Our Lord of Barrocas. Side door. Aveiro.

virtually the same plume-like formation as those of gilded wood which frame the curtains of the lambrequin of John V´s portrait at the end of the library. The frame of the targe at Aveiro is now no longer the simple circle used in the early over-doors. It has taken on the same eccentric baroque form used in the targes of the interior of the library, with even a suggestion of the spiral motifs projecting in broken form the lower part of the frame. The decoration of the Aveiro targe has connections also with the exterior of the library, for below it is a garland very similar to the beautiful one hanging over the entablature of the library portal and it is surmounted by a shell of frilled or ruffled profile, as in the outdoor shield at Coimbra. Finally, to make this composite relationship complete, the base of Aveiro shell evolves into a mask as does the shell below the targe with the royal arms inside the library at Coimbra. This new mask, representing the plump face of a man with curling moustaches, appropriately recalls some of the heads used in the keystones of ground story arcades in the architecture of J.M. Mansart and his school. The lines of the pediments in the small doors at Aveiro, however, have little or no relation to that French style, for they flare inward in the manner of certain of Francesco Borromini´s door and window frames (40). This is then a new Italian element in the design, which Claude Laprade could have learned through the illustrations of Fernando Bibiena´s *Architettura Civile* (41) as well as through contact with a group of Italian architects in Portugal headed by Filippo Juvara, who had recently spent six months in that country. (42)

Very close in spirit and style to the whole composition is a lunette relief set in inside of the wall of the forecourt of the XVII century church of Aveiro.[200] (43) This mutilated sculpture (fig

[200] Without full indication in the text to the church he mentions. It refers to the male convent of the Discalced Carmelites in Aveiro. We are grateful to José Rebocho Cristo, director of the Museum of Santa Joana in Aveiro, for this information, cf. Gonçalves, A. N. (1959) - *Inventário Artístico de Portugal. Distrito de Aveiro.* (pp.

Fig. 65 Detail of a mask inserted into a shell at the bottom of the coat of arms surmounting the portrait of the king John V. Joanine Library. CFT001.12482 © Robert C. Smith. Legado Robert Chester Smith, Fundação Calouste Gulbenkian, Biblioteca de Arte e Arquivos, Lisboa.

Fig. 66 Mask at the Hotel du Carnavelet. Paris. França © Sílvia Ferreira

10), which shows an Infant Saint John the Baptist romping with tiny *putti* in the midst of volutes, is certainly a work of Claude Laprade, for it bears the closest relationship to the *genii* of the over-doors at Coimbra of 1702 and to the figures of the side doors at the Senhor das Barrocas. Further associations with this work are to be found in the formation of the volutes above the figure of the infant saint[201], between which are set two tiny masks quite in the fashion of the minor doorways at Aveiro. The definitions of the fleece of the lamb by means of punch marks brings to mind earlier works of the sculptor and the position of the *putti* embracing the stalks at the bottom of the relief is not without relation to the attitudes of the flying cherubs of the bishop´s tomb at Vista Alegre. Finally, there is a suggestion of Laprade´s early naturalism in the realistic way in which the cedar trees of the background have been rendered.

Although the flavour of this sculpture attains almost the gaiety of a vignette of the XVIII century, the use of the lunette form in an arch above the entrance gate once again shows the influence of French decoration of the XVII century. The motif appears at a number of great houses in Paris, including the Hôtel Carnavalet, which François Mansart rebuilt in 1654, and Cottard´s Hôtel Amelot de Bisseuil, of 1657-1660, with the fine reliefs of the arched portal by Thomas Regnaudin representing *War and Peace* and *Romulus and Remus.* (44)

The date of 1711, which appears on the wall, may or may not be the date of the Carmelite relief. There is reason to believe, however, that the work at Barrocas was done about a decade later, when the church was nearing completion.

127-130). Academia Nacional de Belas-Artes. VI; Neves, A. (1984). *Aveiro. Arte e História.*; *História da Arte em Portugal.* (1986). Edições Alfa. VII.

[201] At the inside portal of the church of the male convent of the Discalced Carmelites.

Fig. 67 Interior wall of the narthex of the Carmelite Church of Aveiro. Relief depicting Saint John the Baptist. © Sílvia Ferreira

Fig. 68 Coat of arms of D. Manuel de Moura Manuel flanked by children. Tomb of D. Manuel de Moura Manuel. Vista Alegre Chapel. Ílhavo. © Sílvia Ferreira

The major doorway of this building[202] has the same composite relation to the decorative elements of the Library of the University of Coimbra that has been noted in regard to the minor portal (fig. 9). In the lower part there occurs an almost exact reproduction of the Coimbra doorframe except that one pair of the Ionic columns is recessed. Here is the identical geometric panelling of the jambs and reveals the same brass scroll with a Latin inscription displayed above the arch (45). Here also are the same brackets below an arch from the soffit of which foliate pendants protrude and an elaborately decorated targe, which although badly broken shows the same confirmation of acanthus, mask, flower garland and spiral wands. Furthermore, at the door of the Senhor das Barrocas can be seen the same miniature masks in the capitals and the identical handling of the lowest member of the entablature found at the Library in Coimbra. Lastly, a piquant analogy exists between the tiny balls set at intervals between the dentils of the doorway at Aveiro and the balls on top of the urns of the portal and on the interior targes at Coimbra.

Small differences exist, for the doorway at the church of the Senhor das Barrocas is not a faithful copy of that of the library of the University of Coimbra. The bird forms have been removed from the brackets at Aveiro and are placed in the spandrels of the arch, which at Coimbra had been left plain. The lowest part of the entablature at Aveiro is enriched by a central projection which carries a mask. The projecting columns at Aveiro, instead of supporting urns on high plinths, as they do at Coimbra, sustain fragments of an arch terminating in scrolls. All the changes and in particular the new position of the columns create a richer and more dramatic effect, which emphasizes the baroque quality of the design.

The composition at Aveiro reaches its climax in the upper section, which has no further relation to the doorway at Coimbra,

[202] Church of Senhor das Barrocas, in Aveiro.

Fig. 69 Relief set in a semicircle on the portal of the Carnavelet Hotel. Paris.

Fig. 70 Column and chapitel of the Church of Our Lord of Barrocas main portal. Aveiro. © Sílvia Ferreira

although there are still links with the style of Claude de Laprade. These reaffirm the attribution of the whole work to that sculptor.

Here he has returned to the vertical arrangement of figures which he had for early employed at the royal monument in Coimbra and at the tomb in Vista Alegre. A pair of female statues, this time representing angels with symbols of the Passion, originally was seated upon fragments of arches over the door. (fig. 11) About a decade ago, however, the image of the left fell off in a storm and was pulverized on the ground below, with the result that only the angel with the towel of St. Veronica remains.[203] This statue very closely resembles the allegories of King Joseph´s monument at Coimbra, especially in the handling of the drapery and in the upward sweep of the hair. The face is more youthful, as befits an angel, suggesting its counterpart of the Bishop´s tomb at Vista Alegre or the allegory of Justice there. Standing upon huge acanthus volutes behind the angelic figures, whom they attend like train bearers, are two vivacious and forcely carved *putti*, statues which like those of the angels show an anatomical knowledge more convincing than that of the early work and a great sense of theatrical arrangement.

This dramatic movement, which begins in the doorframe and is augmented in the statues of the middle zone, comes to its climax in the composition at the top, where once again sprawling genii frame a central decoration interlaced with floral garlands. It is the crowing feature of a design which incorporates a deeply set window whose outer frame has concave angle sections like those of the ground story of Borromini´s Collegio di Propaganda Fide in Rome, of 1647-1644). (fig. 12) (46) Continued in vault form inward to the sunken window itself, this is probably the first example of a

---

[203] Recently this sculpture has also felt off. Editor´s note. The fragments of the two statues are in store at the Museu de Aveiro.

Figs. 71 e 71a. Angel head from the entablature of the portal of the Barrocas Church. Aveiro. Storage of the Museu de Aveiro/ Santa Joana.
© Sílvia Ferreira

Fig. 71 a

Figs. 72 a 74 Fragments of fallen statues from the entablature of the portal of the Church of Senhor das Barrocas. Fragments of a body, the impression of the face of Christ on Veronica's veil, and wings of an angel. © Sílvia Ferreira

Fig. 73

Fig. 74

motif used on several occasions in the Luso-Brazilian architecture of this period (47). This very unusual profile dictates the form of the upper entablature of the doorway. That in turn culminates in a pediment or special design, which like the flaring lines of the lateral doors effectively complements the outline of the window and intensifies the unity of the exterior decoration of the church. The form achieved in the upper part of this doorway, like the winged seraph´s head it enclosures, is strongly Borrominesque and seems to derive from one of the windows of the *piano nobile* of the *Collegio di Propaganda Fide.* (fig. 13) It is not, however, necessary to assume a direct relationship, for the motif of volutes supporting this particular kind of abbreviated pediment, where the apex section projects slightly beyond the rest, was a favourite decorative device among the Italian architects of the generation of Juvara. Extensively imitated in Portugal and Brazil, especially in the so called Pombaline architecture of the second half of the XVIII century (48), this kind of pediment made one of its first appearances in Portugal at the church of the Senhor das Barrocas. The slightly curving cornice of the pediment is repeated in the pedimental fragments on either side of the targe above scroll, which in turn repeat the form of the cornices of the lateral doorways.

The great portal of the church in Aveiro terminates with a high cross set on a base which Laprade with a playful intent that recalls his trick of the castle towers and royal shields of the monument at Coimbra, built of three large dice. The idea comes from the royal arms of Portugal (49), where five shields are arranged in such a way as to suggest the five of dice. Thus, at the very top of this towering portal a final whimsical piece of evidence is provided to support the belief that Claude de Laprade was its author.

The doorway of the church of the Senhor das Barrocas cannot be dated exactly. We have seen that Laprade may have worked in Aveiro as early as 1711 in connection with the relief of St. John the Baptist at the church of *Nossa Senhora do Carmo.*[204] At that time there is no record of his activity in Coimbra, and it is likely to suppose that the sculptor undertook this work before the great design for the library of Coimbra. It is unlikely, however, that the portal of the church of Barrocas precedes in date that of the Library in Coimbra. The latter was set up in 1720. We may then conjecture that those responsible for the building of the church at Aveiro, seeing Laprade´s doorway at Coimbra, commissioned a more elaborate version for their own building, which could have been completed along with the smaller doorways by 1722, when the church was dedicated, or slightly later. The mastery of the sculpture, the brilliant flowing movement and the specifically Italian flavour of some parts of the composition, all argue for the later dating, as does what little is known of the subsequent development of Laprade´s Portuguese career.

The inside of the church of the Senhor das Barrocas, unlike that of the Library at Coimbra, does not repeat the decoration of the exterior. (50) There are, it is true, certain points of connection – the sculptures drapery of the high altar, the garland brackets, the pendants on the woodcarving of the chancel vault, at the base of the pulpits and the summit of the polygonal ceiling of the nave. Finally, there are the groups of *putti* on top of the pulpits and the lion masks with rippled shells at their bases. These slight resemblances, more in subject matter than in style, are counterbalanced by the disparate nature of the frame of the high altar, the treatment of the chancel vault and most of all by the crude figures of popular woodcarving that abound throughout the altarpiece. It may be that this woodwork was in part designed by Laprade and then was carried out by an undistinguished imitator. It is more likely, however, that the whole design is the work of some secondary figure, a clue to whose identity may lie in the tiny male figures seated beneath

[204] Church of the male convent of Discalced Carmelites, in Aveiro.

the column of the high altar, figures which have the air of miniature Atlantids. A similar type and similar gestures appear on the stone base of the pulpit of the parish church of Águada de Cima near Águeda, in the district of Aveiro, a town which belonged in the early XVIII century to the University of Coimbra. (51) For this reason, the same sculptor may have been asked to imitate there the human supporters, flower garlands, shells and targes that are such conspicuous features of Claude Laprade´s work for the University.

During the years following 1716 Claude de Laprade reached the zenith of his career in Portugal, as far as it can now be reconstructed. In his work on the new library of the University of Coimbra he continued to employ the stately French forms of decoration which he had brought with him to Portugal, combining them, as he had previously done in the bishop´s tomb at Vista Alegre, with certain traditional devices absorbed in the country of his adoption. The library reveals, however, a new maturity, expressed in the greater clarity, bordering on austerity, of the exterior design, and in the noble unity of decoration of the interior. At the same time that he was creating this masterpiece Laprade seems to have been experimenting with new forms in the portal of the church of the Senhora das Barrocas at Aveiro. That work, whose basic design is closely related to the doorway of the Library of Coimbra, contains elements derived from the style of Borromini, which Ludovice had brought from Italy when he came to Portugal in 1702, but which he had not applied on a large scale until the beginning of Mafra in 1717. Since this date coincides with the putative dating of the doorway at Aveiro there is every reason to attribute to Laprade an important role in launching the new Italianate style which was to dominate the major constructions of the reign of John V in Portugal and, after 1740, those of the great colony of Brazil.

During the last period of his activity in Portugal Claude de Laprade was to continue to work in this style as one of the foremost designers of the grandiose altarpieces of gilded and polychromed wood, which are among the most characteristic products of the Joanine period of Portuguese art.

Notes

(1) Teófilo Braga, *História da Universidade de Coimbra*, vol. II, p. 151. We wish also to refer the reader to our article "Early works of Claude Laprade and the style Louis XIV in Portugal", *Gazette des Beaux-Arts*, October 1954, pp. 163-190.

(2) *"Depois da paz de Utrecht em 1715 começou este Reino a respirar e D. João o 5.° pôde deitar as vistas sobre as sciências e boas artes*[205]*".* Cyrilo Wolkmar Machado, Collecção de Memorias, relativas às vidas dos pintores, e architectos, e gravadores portugueses (...), Lisboa, na Imp. de Victorino Rodrigues da Silva, 1823, p. 188.

(3) The existing library, much of which had been collected by order of Philip III of Spain, who reigned as Philip II of Portugal in 1604, under the supervision of the Rector Francisco de Castro (1605-1611). See Teófilo Braga, *op. cit.*, vol. II, pp. 816, 819. It was housed in one of the new rooms of the *Gerais*, for which Laprade carved a symbolic over-door.

(4) Bernardo Brito Botelho, *História Breve de Coimbra*, Lisboa, 1733, p. 25, p. 48 in the 2nd annotated edition by A.F. Barata, Lisboa, Imprensa Nacional, 1873. This was during the rectorate of D. Nuno da Silva Teles II (1715-1719), who was the second son of D. Nuno´s older brother, D. Manuel, third Marquis of Alegrete. See António Caetano de Sousa *Memórias historicas, e genealógicas dos grandes de Portugal*, Lisboa, Na Regia Officina Sylviana, e da Academia Real, 1755, p. 68-69. The plan was published as part of the illustration of our article "The early works of Claude Laprade (...)", fig. 2.

5) *Guia de Portugal*, vol. III, tomo I, p. 278.

6) Bernardo Botelho, *op. cit.*, p. 23.

7) For a discussion of Mafra and the Patriarchal church, see my[206] "J. F. Ludovice, An Eighteenth-Century Architect in Portugal", *Art Bulletin*, vol. XVIII, n.' 3, setembro, 1936, pp. 273-370.

8) In the archive of the University of Coimbra there remain nine volumes of a set of records originally containing eleven. These are manuscript accounts known as *Obras da Livraria*. They indicate the expenses began with the excavation of the foundations of the library building on April 30, 1717. Stone from the quarries of Ilhastro (also from Portunhos and Ançã) is mentioned in May, as well as the name of João Roiz de Almeida, master carpenter of the University, who seems to have directed much of the work. In the Autumn of 1717, brick was being brought from Sangalhos; the master locksmith of Coimbra, Bernardo Vieira, was making the

[205] In Portuguese.

[206] By mistake Smith refers the text about Claude Laprade.

iron bars for the windows of the lower story of the library; and the woodcarver Manuel Moreira was paid 4$000 reis on Nov. 27, for a plan of this area of the building. Chestnut wood was being cut until January, 1719, under the direction of Almeida. In December of that year, they were making the bookshelves of chestnut and pine, under the direction of Master Gaspar Ferreira. They were also erecting a crane for lifting the lintel and columns of the doorway, which were set in place on April 16, 1720, again under the Ferreira´s supervision. On May 25 of this year, wood was being prepared for the roof, and by September, stucco was being mixed for the ceiling. Here the history is interrupted because of the two missing volumes of accounts. It was during this period, however, in 1723 that António Simões Ribeiro and Vicente Nunes of Lisbon were paid for painting the allegorical decorations on the ceilings of the three rooms of the library.[207] In February 1725, glass was being provided by Albano dos Reis Salgado for four large windows and João Roiz de Almeida had been paid for carving the ornaments of the balcony railing. According to these accounts, which go to 1728, 47:596$822 rs. were spent on the work from a royal gift of 49:140$200 rs. Florêncio Mago Barreto Feio lists the total expense at 66:622$129 rs., *Memória histórica e descriptiva á cêrca da biblioteca da universidade de Coimbra*, Coimbra, 1857, pp. 25-36.

9) José Ramos Bandeira, "Universidade de Coimbra- Paço das Escolas e Casa dos Mellos", *O Instituto*, vol. 92, 2.ª parte, Coimbra, Gráfica de Coimbra, 1947, pp. 457-700, *Guia de Portugal*, Biblioteca Nacional de Lisboa, Lisboa, 1927, vol. III, p. 278.

10) More suggestive of the style of Ludovice is the campanile in the northwest corner of the University courtyard, the plan of which is known to have been obtained in Lisbon. It was constructed between 1728 and 1732, Florêncio Mago Barreto Feio, *op. cit.*, p. 37.

11) Represented in my article[208], "Early works of Claude Laprade (...)", fig. 9.

12) *Ibidem,* fig. 15.

13) Marot´s arch was apparently intended to serve as a city gate, cf. Ernest Wasmuth, Das ornamentwerk des Daniel Marot, Berlin, 1892, p. 26. The library façade is also related to the one-store constructions at the entrance to the courtyards of the Parisian *hôtels particuliers*[209], where an arch between coupled columns was a common arrangement in the early XVIII century. See Louis Hautecoeur, *Histoire de l´architecture classique en France*, vol. III, Paris, 1950, pp. 186-189. The motif in French art can be traced back to an engraving of J.A. Du Cerceau of 1534, Henry de Geymüller, Les Du Cerceau, leur vie et leur oeuvre, Paris, Librairie de l'Art, 1887, fig. 19.

14) See[210] my "Early works of Claude Laprade (...)", fig. 1.

15) *Ibidem*, fig. 5, 6 and 7.

---

[207] See Raggi, G. (2018). À conquista da sabedoria: a pintura de quadratura e o programa iconográfico da Biblioteca Joanina. *Boletim da Biblioteca Geral da Universidade de Coimbra*, Imprensa da Universidade de Coimbra 48, 37-90.

[208] Smith quotes by mistake his article about Ludovice, when referring to his text about Laprade.

[209] In French.

[210] See note 27.

16) In France at this time the rosette of the Ionic capital was experimentally replaced by cocks, *fleurs-de-lis*[211] and the symbols of the great French orders of knighthood, Louis Hautecoeur, *op. cit.*, vol. II, pp. 352-354.

17) Being replaced by a monotonous use of cannon mouths under Mannerist influence from Spain. The spouts at the chapel of Versailles (ca. 1700-1710) terminate in the mouths of monsters.

18) Lest Claude Laprade be given credit for too many innovations, it should be remembered that he was working in Portugal at a time coinciding with a revival, principally in woodcarving, of the fantastic birds and animals of Manueline decoration. This tendency was part of what I have called the national style of woodcarving, which flourished between 1675 and 1725. See Robert C. Smith, "The Portuguese woodcarved retable, 1600-1750", *Belas-Artes*, 2.ª série, n.º 2, 1950, pp. 21-27.

19) According to D. António Caetano de Sousa, nineteen triumphal arches were erected, apparently of ephemeral materials, by the guilds and foreign colonies between the royal palace and the cathedral for the procession on December 22, 1705, *História genealógica da casa real portuguesa,* Lisboa, vol. VIII, 1741, p. 64. One of these, the arch for the English, was designed by Carlos Gimac, Francisco Marques de Sousa Viterbo, *Diccionário histórico e documental dos architectos, engenheiros e constructores portugueses ou a serviço de Portugal,* vol. I, Lisboa, 1899, p. 424.

Since the tiles of the Third Order of St. Francis are not dated, it is also possible that they may represent the entrance into Lisbon on February 12, 1729, of the Prince of Brazil, the future Joseph I, and his Spanish bride, Mariana Victoria de Bourbon[212], D. António Caetano de Sousa, in describing their procession, mentions only briefly the triumphal arches, describing none of them, *op. cit.*, vol. VIII, p. 300. If this interpretation is the correct one, then the unidentified arch here attributed to Claude de Laprade would belong to a later period of activity, when the sculptor was designing altarpieces in Lisbon.[213]

20) This inscription was called to my attention by R.C. Taylor, in a letter of June 23, 1953.

---

[211] In French.

[212] About these tiles, see Basto M. (2005) - *Os azulejos da Ordem terceira de São Francisco de Salvador: uma representação simbólica da cultura política barroca portuguesa no Brasil durante o reinado de D. João V.* (Tese de doutoramento apresentada à Pontifícia Universidade Católica do Rio de Janeiro).

[213] The original note written by Smith confused the wedding arches of D. João V with those built for the marriage of his son D. José I. We have chosen not to include this comment in the text, because this passage would certainly not have passed Smith's or a colleague's review to the manuscript.

If there are brief comments about the wedding arches of King João V, of which the best source is still the *História Genealógica da Casa Real Portuguesa* written by António Caetano de Sousa and the booklet on the arche of the English. As mentioned above, nothing can be found in the contemporary bibliography about the wedding arches of King José. In the cloister of the convent of the Third Order of São Francisco, in Salvador da Bahia, Brazil, there is a set of figurative tiles whose scenes represent the entry into Lisbon of the newlyweds D. José and D. Mariana Vitória, where there are triumphal arches. However, these representations have long been classified as imaginary.

21) See note 7. Botelho called it a "grandioso portico", *op. cit.*, p. 231.

22) *Ibidem.*

23) The Library of Coimbra was greatly admired by one of the first foreigners to write extensively on Portuguese art. Count Atanazy Raczynski, Polish minister to Portugal, found it "la plus belle, la plus richement ornée, que j´aie jamais visitée", *Les arts en Portugal,* Paris, 1846, p. 471. This and other Portuguese XVIII century libraires enjoyed considerable fame, even among Spaniards, who were generally indifferent to things in the neighboring kingdom. One of them José Martínez Moreno, wrote from Lisbon on May 12, 1772 "*en Coimbra vimos la Biblioteca, y Aulas de Universidad...a cuya vista deven arriconnarse a las de nuestra España. En punto de Librerias es mui profuso el genio destos Naturales; pues en cualquiera Combento [sic] se halla mucha abundancia, y mucha curiosidade, Es singular en esta parte la del de Mafra*", Fidelino de Figueiredo, "Viajantes espanhoes em Portugal", *Boletins da Faculdade de Filosofia, Ciências e Letras da Universidade de São Paulo*, vol. LXXXIV, 1947, p. 13. Similarly, Charles d´Hautefort praised the monastic libraires of Lisbon, which in the early XIX century contained from 30,000 to 50,000 volumes, *Coup-d´oeil sur Lisbonne et Madrid em 1814,* Paris, 1820, pp. 36-48-49 and 51.

With the suppression of the monastic communities, in 1834[214], these books were incorporated in the public collections and most of the rich interiors were gradually dismantled. Two outstanding examples, however, have survived. These are the libraries at the church of Santíssimo Sacramento, Paulistas[215], and the former convent of Mafra. Comparisons can be made with the fine monastic libraires of Central Europe, F. Hepner, "Libraries of the Baroque. Survey of examples in Bavaria and Austria", *Architectural Review*, vol. CVII, n.° 640, Apr. 1950, pp. 255-260.

24) The comparison derives from Albrecht Haupt, who wrote in 1895, *die von Joao V neu erbaute herrliche Bibliothek, sin Seiten stuck zu der Fisher von Erlach in Wien*, in *Die Baukunst der Renaissance in Portugal,* Frankfurt, vol. I, p. 91. For a description of the Hofbibliothek, see Hans Seldmayer, *Osterreichische Barok Architektur, 1600-1740*, Vienna, 1930, p. 75, fig. 60.

25) Robert C. Smith, "Portuguese baroque woodcarving", in *Magazine of Art*, vol. 43, n.° 6, Oct. 1950, pp. 218-320.

26) See note 7.

27) See also my "Early works of Claude Laprade and the style Louis XIV in Portugal (...)" fig. 9.

28) The portrait is thought to be the work of the Milanese painter Agostino Binetti[216], Augusto Mendes Simões de Castro, *Guia histórico do viajante em Coimbra e arredores*, Coimbra, 1867, p. 176. Vergílio Correia has found that Binetti was

---

[214] 1835 in the original. The correct date is 1834.

[215] Today the parish church of Saint Catherine of Alexandria.

[216] The authorship of this portrait of D. João V was attributed, with more solid arguments, by Ayres de Carvalho to the painter Domenico Duprá, see Carvalho, A. (1960) - *D. João V e a arte do seu tempo* (p. 225). Author´s edition. I., reaffirmed years later (1994) in his text: Retrato de D. João V. (pp. 256-259). In Nuno S. (ed.). *A pintura em Portugal ao tempo de D. João V 1706-1750. Joanni V Magnifico.* IPPAR.

living in Lisbon as late as 1741 at the end of Calçada do Combro, cf. Vergílio Correia *Artistas italianos* em Portugal: século XVIII (1ª. metade), *Biblos Revista da Faculdade de Letras da Universidade de Coimbra*. Coimbra, vol. VIII, 1932, p. 128, where he was employed as a designer of stage settings, see Emilio Lavagnino, *Il genio Italiano all´estero. Gli artisti in Portogallo*, Roma, 1940, pp. 133 and 163. Beneath the royal portrait there is the inscription:

"Regia, quem cernis, speculum tibi praestat imago:
In Speculo totum, quod capit aula vides,
Quaeque augusta patent, Ionannis Ordine Quintus
Condidit: aeternum principe vivat opus".

29) It is pertinent to note that armillary spheres appear on the banners of the trumpeting genii of the title page of the 1654 edition of the statues of the University, and an owl is placed beside the seated figure symbolizing the institution.

30) *Nouvelles Chemiée [sic] faittes en plusier [sic] endroits de la Hollande*, Ernest Wasmuth, *op. cit.*, p. 146. Very similar pseudo-Chinese decorations can be seen on the choir stalls of the former Convent of Jesus, at Aveiro.

31) Vergílio Correia e A. Nogueira Gonçalves, *Inventário Artístico de Portugal. Cidade de Coimbra*, vol. II, Lisboa, 1947, p. 92. The polychromed wood-carved drapery held back by flying putti on either side of the altarpiece is almost exactly like that of the portrait of John V at the library in Coimbra, Ibidem, fig. CXXXIV.

32) This is another characteristic of the Louis XIV decoration. The motif was engraved on many occasions, for example in Balthasar Moncornet´s *Livre nouveau de toutes sortes d´ouvrages d´orfèvres*, Paris, [about 1670], reprinted in London, 1888, fig. 5.

33) The sacristy is a fine example of interior polychromy as practiced in Portugal in the early years of the reign of John V. Around the center of the wall runs a broad band of gilded wood sculpture, incorporating a group of brilliantly colored paintings. Below this band there is a dado of blue and white pictorial tiles. Above it the vault is decorated with massive garlands and arabesques in vivid tones upon white plaster.

34) Marques Gomes, *Memórias de Aveiro,* Aveiro, 1875, pp. 101-102. The church is located at some distance from the center of the then town on the road to Esgueira. The Portuguese words of the invocations can be translated as "Our Lord of the Valleys".

35) The image, known as the Senhor Jesus de Bouças, is connected with the *Volto Santo de Lucca*. The cult was taken to Brazil in the XVIII century, where it thrives at Congonhas do Campo in Minas Gerais, Robert C. Smith, "Colonial Architecture of Minas Gerais", *Art Bulletin*, vol. XXI, 1939, p. 138.

36) Alberto Souto (1952). Aveiro (p. 22). *Arte Antiga em Portugal.* Marques Abreu. I.

37) Reynaldo dos Santos, *L´art portugais. XVI congrès international d´Histoire de l´art,* Lisbonne-Porto, 1949, p. 27.

38) *Ibidem*.

39) The attribution is made in Alberto Souto, *op. cit.*, p. 22.

40) *Ibidem*. The resemblance between the main portal and that of the Library at Coimbra had been noted by Carlos de Passos in 1944, *Guia de Portugal,* vol. III, p. 495, but without any attempt at attribution.

41) Especially the frame of the blind niche of the first stage of the tower of S. Andrea delle Fratte in Rome, designed in 1653, cf. Eberhard Hempel, *Francesco Borromini*, Vienna, 1924, fig. 109.

42) First published in Parma in 1711.

43) Filippo Juvara (1674-76-1736) came to Portugal in November 1719 and remained there for six months, making drawings for additions to the Royal Palace in Lisbon and for the Patriarchal church, some of which are at the library in Turin.[217] For a consideration of other Italian working in Lisbon for John V, see Lavagnino, *op. cit.*, pp. 85-123.[218]

44) Founded in 1613 by the discalced Carmelites, the building was completed in 1643, Passos, *op. cit.*, p. 494.

45) These are illustrated in Georges Pillement, *Les Hôtels du Marais*, Paris, 1948, figs. XXXV and XLV.

46) The scroll at the church of Barrocas is inscribed with the words:

> "Domus Mea Domus Orationis Vocabitur
> Pulsate et Aperietur Vobis"

That of the Library of the University of Coimbra reads:

> "Lusiadae, Hanc Vobis Sapientia Condidit Arcem
> Directores Libri: Miles et Arma Labor".

A similar scroll is placed over the arche on the inside.

47) This design, which suggest an upper section of an irregular octagon, was a favourite device of Borromini for heightening the tension of his architecture. He seems to have used it first in one of the apartments of the Oratorio di S. Filippo Neri in Rome and in the niches of the ground story of the façade (1637-1640). It appears in the interior balconies of the University church of S. Ivo della Sapienza (1642-1660). In the minor portal of the Augustinian nunnery church of S. Maria de´ Sette Dolori (1652) and, finally, in the lateral niches of the lower story of Borromini´s best known work, the façade of S. Carlo alle Quattro Fontane

---

217 An analysis of the circumstances of Juvara's coming to Portugal and the architectural projects he has designed for the King João V can be found in the recent work by Raggi, G. (2020) - *O projeto de D. João V. Lisboa Ocidental, Mafra e o urbanismo cenográfico de Filippo Juvara*. Caleidoscópio.

218 Recent studies on Italian artists who worked in Portugal for King João V have increased knowledge of the political, cultural and economic circumstances of their movements, and have promoted new analyses and debates on what had hitherto been written on the subject.

(1662-1667). All these Roman buildings are illustrated in Hempel, *op. cit.,* fig. 37, 39, 75, 79 and 123.

48) This kind of opening appears in the doors of the chancel of the church of Menino Deus (see note 37) and in the porch of the Lisbon church of Our Lady of Necessidades, built in 1745-1750 on plans of Caetano Tomaz de Sousa. It was used for a vaulted passageway adjacent to the late XVIII century church of Sta. Tereza in Recife in Brazil. The motif was also frequently employed for the lintels of the ground story of large houses in both Portugal and Brazil.

49) I have written briefly of this style in my "Palacio de los gobernadores de Gran-Pará", *Annales del Instituto de arte americano e investigaciones estéticas*, Buenos Aires, vol. 4, 1951, pp. 9-26.

50) Both were in part the product of royal largess and thus entitled to display the royal arms. The building of the Senhor das Barrocas was aided by a contribution from taxes, Marques Gomes, *op. cit.*, pp. 101-102.

51) Photographs of the interior are published in Alberto Souto, *op. cit.,* fig. 34 and 35, and of the high altar, in my "The Portuguese Woodcarved Retable (...)", fig. 25.

52) *Guia de Portugal*, vol. II, p. 576.

Bibliography

Studies

A arte em Portugal no século XVIII. Congresso Internacional de Estudos em Homenagem a André Soares (1973-1974). *Bracara Augusta.* XVII e XVIII.

Almeida, M. L. (1971) - *Artes e Ofícios em Documentos da Universidade.* Imprensa de Coimbra Lta. II.

Almeida, M. L. (1937) - *Documentos da Reforma Pombalina* (1771-1782). Universidade de Coimbra. I.

Almeida, O. T. (2013). Manoel da Silveira Cardozo (1911-1985) – Um historiador picoense nos Estados Unidos. *Boletim do Núcleo Cultural da Horta.*

Almeida, A. J. op. (2005). A mobilidade do impressor quinhentista Pedro de Mariz. In Natália M. F-A. (ed.). *Artistas e Artífices e a sua mobilidade no mundo de expressão portuguesa: actas do VII Colóquio Luso-Brasileiro de História da Arte.* CEPESE- Universidade do Porto.

Alves, A. (1982). A actividade de Gaspar Ferreira em terras do interior Beirão. *Mundo da Arte.* 6.

Alves, A. (1980). Artistas e Artífices nas Dioceses de Lamego e Viseu. *Revista Beira Alta.* XXXIX, facs 3 e 4.

Alves, A. (1959). A Santa Casa da Misericórdia de Mangualde. *Revista Beira Alta.* XVIII.

Girão, A., Correia, V. e Soares, T. S. (1939) - *Coimbra e Arredores.* Comissão Municipal de Turismo.

Bandeira, J. R. (1947) - *Universidade de Coimbra. Edifícios do Corpo Central e Casa dos Melos* I. Casa do Castelo.

Bazin, G. (1960). La Bibliothèque la plus fausteuse que j´aie jamais vu. *Connaissance des Arts*, 100.

Botelho, Bernardo de Brito. (1873) - *Historia Breve de Coimbra.* (2.ª ed.). Imprensa Nacional.

Braga, T. (1892-1902) - *História da Universidade de Coimbra nas suas relações com a instrução pública.* Academia Real das Ciências.

Braga, T. (1894) - *Dom Francisco de Lemos e a Reforma da Universidade de Coimbra.* Typographia da Academia Real das Sciencias.

Bric-à Brac. Notas Históricas e Arqueológicas. (1926). Livraria Fernando Machado editora.

Carvalho, J. M. T. (1914). Pedro de Mariz e a Livraria da Universidade de Coimbra. *Boletim bibliográfico da Biblioteca da Universidade de Coimbra*. 1.

Carvalho, A. (1962) - *D. João V e a Arte do Seu Tempo*. Edição de autor. II.

Carvalho, A. (1964). Novas revelações para a história do Barroco em Portugal. II-O mestre das gloriosas máquinas douradas da Lisboa setecentista. O artista Claude de Laprade (1682-1738). separata de *Belas-Artes*. 20.

Carvalho, A. (1994) - Retrato de D. João V. In Nuno S. (ed). *A pintura em Portugal ao tempo de D. João V 1706-1750. Joanni V Magnifico*. IPPAR.

Castro, A.M.S. (1880) - *Guia Historico do Viajante em Coimbra* (2.ª edição). Imprensa da Universidade.

Coelho, T. C. (2014) - *Os Nunes Tinoco, uma dinastia de arquitectos régios dos séculos XVII e XVIII*. (Tese de doutoramento em História da Arte, Faculdade de Ciências Sociais e Humanas da Universidade NOVA de Lisboa). I.

Correia, V. (1932). Artistas italianos em Portugal: século XVIII (1ª. metade). *Biblos Revista da Faculdade de Letras da Universidade de Coimbra*. VIII.

Correia, V. (1946) - Obras Antigas da Universidade. In *Obras*. Por Ordem da Universidade de Coimbra. I.

Correia, V. e Gonçalves, A. N. (1947) - *Inventário Artístico de Portugal. Cidade de Coimbra*. Academia Nacional de Belas-Artes.

Costa, A.C. (1868-1869) - *Corografia Portugueza e Descripçam Topografica do Famoso Reyno de Portugal*. (2.ª edição). Typ. de Domingos Gonçalves Gouveia. II.

Costa, L. X. (1934) - *As belas-artes plásticas em Portugal durante o século XVIII*. J. Rodrigues & Co.ª.

Das ornamentwerk des Daniel Marot. (1892) - Wasmuth, E.

Discripçam do arco triunfal que a naçam Ingleza mandou levantar (...). (1708). Officina de Valentim da Costa Deslandes.

Espanca, T. (1972). Convento de S. Paulo da Serra de Ossa. *A Cidade de Évora*. XXIX 55.

Feio, F. M. B. (1857) - *Memória Histórica e Descriptiva à cerca da Biblioteca da Universidade de Coimbra*. Imprensa da Universidade.

Ferreira, S. (2017). From stone to wood: Claude Laprade (c. 1675-1738) and his journey from Provence to Portugal. In Kathryn W., Jessica D., Matej K. (eds). *Artists and migration 1400-1850, Britain, Europe and beyond*. Cambridge Scholars Publishing.

Ferreira, S. (2002) - *A talha dourada do altar-mor da igreja de Santa Catarina, em Lisboa. A intervenção do entalhador Santos Pacheco*. (Dissertação de mestrado em História da Arte, Universidade Lusíada de Lisboa).

Ferreira, S. (2022). Gold on Blue in Philadelphia. Robert C. Smith and the Installation of the 'Portuguese Chapel' at the Samuel S. Fleisher Art Memorial. *RIHA Journal* (Novembro).

Ferreira, S. (2015) - Reflexos em vermelho e ouro. Chinoiserie e talha ou a construção de um modelo de renovação artística. In Luís F. B., Vítor S. (eds.). *Património Cultural Chinês em Portugal*. Centro Científico e Cultural de Macau.

Ferreira, S. (2019) - Claude Laprade: um escultor do Barroco entre a Provença e Portugal. In Paulo A. F., Ana Paula A. (eds.). *Lisboa Plural: 1147-1910*. Museu de Lisboa.

Ferreira, S., Rosada, M. (2023) - A policromia poliédrica. Do douramento à *chinoiserie* no barroco luso-brasileiro. In Manuel G. L., Francisco J. H. G. (eds.). *Color y Ornamento. Estudios sobre polícromía en el mundo ibérico (s. XVII y XVIII)*. Universidad de Granada.

Ferreira-Alves, N. M. (2001) - *A escola de talha portuense e a sua influência no norte de Portugal*. Edições Inapa.

Figueiroa, F. C. (1937) - *Memórias da Universidade de Coimbra*. Por Ordem da Universidade de Coimbra.

Figueirôa-Rêgo, J. (2013) - Das instâncias académicas de Coimbra ao Santo Ofício e à Mesa da Consciência e Ordens: in(ter)dependencia(s), sociabilidades e interesses. In Fátima F., Hermínia V. V., Mafalda S. C. *Centros Periféricos de Poder na Europa do Sul (Séculos XII-XVIII)*, (eds.). Colibri-CIDEHUS/UÉ.

Figueiredo, F. (1947). Viajantes espanhoes em Portugal. *Boletins da Faculdade de Filosofia, Ciências e Letras*. LXXXIV, 3.

Fonseca, F. T. (2007). The Social and Cultural Roles of the University of Coimbra (1537-1820). Some Considerations. *e-Journal of Portuguese History*, n.° 5 https://www.brown.edu/Departments/Portuguese_Brazilian_Studies/ejph/html/issue9/html/ffonseca_main.html.

França, J. A. (1965) - *Une ville de lumiere, la Lisbonne de Pombal*. Publicações da École Pratique des Hautes Études.

Garcia, P. Q. (1923) - *Documentos para as Biografias dos Artistas de Coimbra*. Imprensa da Universidade.

Marques Gomes. (1875) - *Memórias de Aveiro*. Typ. Commercial.

Geymüller, H. (1887) - *Les Du Cerceau, leur vie et leur œuvre*. J. Rouam.

Gonçalves, A. A. (1899) - Breve Noção sobre a História das Ceramicas em Coimbra. In Charles P. (ed.). *Estudo Chimico e Technologico sobre a Ceramica Portugueza Moderna*. Imprensa Nacional.

Gonçalves, A. N. (1959) - *Inventário Artístico de Portugal. Distrito de Aveiro*. Academia Nacional de Belas-Artes. VII.

Gonçalves, F. (1971-1972). Uma Obra Notável de Francisco Machado. *Bracara Augusta*. XXV-XXVI.

Gschwend, A. (2015). Olisipo, *Emporium Nobilissimum*: global consumption in renaissance Lisbon. In AnneMarie G., K. J. P. L. (eds). *The global city on the streets of the renaissance*. Paul Holberton Publishing.

Haupt, A. (s.d.) - *A arquitetura da renascença em Portugal*. J. Rodrigues Livreiros Editores.

Hautecoeur, L. (1950) - *Histoire de l´architecture classique en France*. Picard. III.

Hautefort C. (1820) - *Coup-d´oeil sur Lisbonne et Madrid en 1814*. Delauney.

Hempel, E. (1924) - *Francesco Borromini*. Schroll.

Hepner, F., (1950) - Libraries of the Baroque in Bavaria and Austria. *Architectural Review*. CVII, 640.

História da Arte em Portugal. (1986) - Publicações Alfa. VII.

Hobson, A. (1970) - *Great Libraries*. Weidenfeld & Nicolson.

Johnson, E. D. (1965) - *A History of Libraires in the Western World*. Scarecrow Press.

Lavagnino, E. (1940) - *Il genio Italiano all´estero. Gli artisti in Portogallo*. La Libreria dello Stato.

López-Salazar, A. (2017) - Una oligarquía eclesiástica en Portugal durante el antiguo régimen: catedráticos, canónigos e inquisidores. *Librosdelacorte.es MONOGRÁFICO*. 6, 9.

Machado, C. W. (1823) - *Collecção de Memorias, relativas às vidas dos pintores, e architectos, e gravadores portugueses (...)*. Imp. de Victorino Rodrigues da Silva.

Masson, A. (1972) - *Le décor des bibliothèques*. Doz.

Mendes, P., Fiolhais, C. (2013) - *Biblioteca Joanina, Universidade de Coimbra*. Imprensa da Universidade de Coimbra.

Moncornet, Balthasar. (1888) - *Livre nouveau de toutes sortes d´ouvrages d´orfèvres*. c.1670. Bernard Quaritch.

Mourão, C. (2009) - Sala do Senado. História e Iconografia. In Teresa P. (ed.). *Sala do Senado*. Assembleia da República-divisão de edições.

Neto, M. J. (2022) - *Arquitetura Medieval Portuguesa. O olhar da americana Georgiana G. King em 1935*. Caleidoscópio.

Neves, Amaro (1984) - *Aveiro. Arte e História*. ADERAV.

Pais, A. N., Pacheco, A., Coroado, J. (2007) - *Cerâmica de Coimbra: do século XVI-XX*. INAPA.

Pillement, G. (1948) - *Les Hôtels du Marais*. Editions Terra.

Pimentel, A. F. (2005) - António Canevari e a torre da Universidade de Coimbra. In Natália M. F-A. (ed.). *Artistas e Artífices e a sua mobilidade no mundo de expressão portuguesa: actas do VII Colóquio Luso-Brasileiro de História da Arte*. CEPESE-Universidade do Porto.

Pimentel, A. F. (2002) - *Arquitectura e Poder. O Real edifício de Mafra*. Livros Horizonte.

Pimentel, A. F. (2000) - Cidade do saber/ cidade do poder: a arquitectura da reforma. In Ana C. A. (ed.). *O Marquês de Pombal e a Universidade*. Imprensa da Universidade de Coimbra.

Pimentel, A. F. (2011) - A Biblioteca da Universidade e os seus espaços. In A. E M.A. (ed.). *Tesouros da Biblioteca Geral da Universidade de Coimbra*. Imprensa da Universidade de Coimbra.

Pimentel, A. F. (2017) - Do convento de Mafra ao real edifício. *Monumentos*. 35.

Pimentel, A. F. (2013) - Do Portugal exótico ao exotismo: o fenómeno da *Chinoiserie* em Portugal. In Alexandra C. (ed.). *O exótico nunca está em casa? A China na faiança e no azulejo portugueses (séculos XVII-XVIII)*. DGPC.

Pimentel, A. F. (1989) - Gaspar Ferreira. In José F. P. (ed.). *Dicionário da arte barroca em Portugal*. Presença.

Pimentel, A.F. (1996). Manuel da Silva e a difusão do barroco nas Beiras. *Oficinas regionais. Actas do VI simpósio luso-espanhol de história da arte,* Tomar, Instituto Politécnico de Tomar.

Pimentel, H. (2018) - *Plantas centralizadas na cidade de Aveiro: a Capela do Senhor das Barrocas (1722 - 1732)*. (Dissertação de Mestrado em Arquitetura, Faculdade de Ciências e Tecnologia da Universidade de Coimbra).

Portela, M. (2020). O mestre de obras de arquitetura Gaspar Ferreira e o convento dos dominicanos da Batalha. *Jornal da Golpilheira* (Jan.-Fev).

Proença, R. (1944) - *Guia de Portugal*. Biblioteca Nacional de Lisboa.

"Professor Doutor Cónego Avelino de Jesus da Costa (1908-2000). (2007). *Revista de História da Sociedade e da Cultura*. 6.

Rackzinski, A. (1846) - *Les arts en Portugal: lettres adressées a la société artistique et scientifique de Berlin et accompagnées de documents*. Jules Renouard et C.ie.

Apollo (1973). XCVII (Abril), 134.

Raggi, G. (2018). À conquista da sabedoria: a pintura de quadratura e o programa iconográfico da Biblioteca Joanina. *Boletim da Biblioteca Geral da Universidade de Coimbra*. 48.

Raggi, G. (2020) - *O projeto de D. João V. Lisboa Ocidental, Mafra e o urbanismo cenográfico de Filippo Juvara*. Caleidoscópio.

Russel-Wood, A.J.R. (2000) - Robert Chester Smith: investigador e historiador. In Jorge R. e Manuel C. (eds.). *Robert C. Smith (1912-1975). A investigação em história de arte*. Fundação Calouste Gulbenkian.

Saldanha S. C. (2010) - A escultura em São Vicente de Fora: projecto, campanhas e autores. In Sandra C. S. (ed.). *Mosteiro de São Vicente de Fora. Arte e História*. Centro Cultural do Patriarcado de Lisboa.

Santos, D. G. (2013) - *Azulejaria de fabrico coimbrão (1699-1801), Artífices e artistas. Cronologia. Iconografia*. (Tese de doutoramento em História da Arte Portuguesa, Faculdade de Letras da Universidade do Porto) I.

Santos Simões, J. M. (2010) - *Azulejaria em Portugal no século XVIII*, (edição atualizada por Maria Alexandra Gago da Câmara, da obra de 1979). Fundação Calouste Gulbenkian.

Santos, R. (1949) - *L´art portugais. XVI congrès international d´Histoire de l´art*, Lisbonne-Porto.

Seldmayer, H. (1930) - *Osterreichische Barok Architektur, 1600-1740*. Dr. Benno Filser Verlag.

Smith, R. C. (1966). A new museum of tiles in Lisbon. *Antiques*. 98, 6.

Smith, R. C (1963) - *A Talha em Portugal*. Livros Horizonte.

Smith, R. C. (1968). Azulejos of Cascais. *The Journal of the American Portuguese Cultural Society*. II, 4.

Smith, R. C. (1968) - *Cadeirais de Portugal*. Livros Horizonte.

Smith, R. C. (1968) - Ceramics: the Tiles. In *The Art of Portugal: 1500-1800*.Weidenfeld and Nicolson.

Smith, R. C. (1939). Colonial Architecture of Minas Gerais. *Art Bulletin*. XXI.

Smith, R. C. (1973) - *Congonhas do Campo*. Agir.

Smith, R. C. (1972). Dois Estudos Beneditinos. *Boletim da Academia Nacional de Belas-Artes*. 27.

Smith, R. C. (1954). Early works of Claude Laprade and the style Louis XIV in Portugal. *Gazette des Beaux-Arts* (Outubro).

Smith R. C. (1936). Frederico Ludovice an eighteenth century architect in Portugal. *The Art Bulletin*. 18, 3.

Smith, R. C. (1968) - *Fr. Cipriano da Cruz, Escultor de Tibães*. Livraria Civilização.

Smith, R. C. (1973). French Models for Portuguese Tiles. *Apollo*. 97, 134.

Smith, R, C. (1970) - *Marceliano de Araújo, escultor bracarense*. Nelita Editora.

Smith, R. C. (1966) - *Nicolau Nasoni, Arquitecto do Porto*. Livros Horizonte.

Smith, R. C. (1973). O pintor Manuel da Silva na Universidade de Coimbra. *O Comércio do. Porto*. 291, 23 de outubro.

Smith, R. C. (1951). Palacio de los gobernadores de Gran-Pará. *Annales del Instituto de arte americano e investigaciones estéticas*. 4.

Smith, R, C. (1950). Portuguese Baroque Woodcarving. *Magazine of Art*. 43, 6.

Smith, R. C. (1964). Portuguese Church Tables. *The Connoisseur*. CLVII, 631.

Smith, R. C. (1975). Some Lisbon Tiles in Estremoz. *The Journal of the American Portuguese Cultural Society*. IX, 2.

Smith, R. C. (1968) - *The Art of Portugal (1500-1800)*. Weidenfeld and Nicolson.

Smith, R. C. (1973). The Building of Mafra. *Apollo* (Abril).

Smith, R. C. (1973). The furniture of Anthony G. Quervelle. *Antiques*. Parte I: maio de 1973, vol. 103, n° 5; parte II: julho de 1973, vol. 104, n° 1; Parte III: agosto de 1973, vol. 104, n° 2; parte IV: janeiro de 1974, vol. 105, n° 1; parte V: março de 1974, vol. 105, n° 3.

Smith, R. C. (1950). The Portuguese woodcarved retable, 1600-1750. *Belas-Artes*. 2.ª série, 2.

Smith, R. C. (1970). Três Estudos Bracarenses. *Belas Artes*. 2.ª série, 24-26.

Sousa, A. C. (1755) - *Memórias historicas, e genealógicas dos grandes de Portugal*. Na Regia Officina Sylviana, e da Academia Real.

Sousa, A. C. (2007) - *História genealógica da casa real portuguesa* (edição da Academia Portuguesa da História e QuidNovi). VIII (1741).

Visconde de Villa Maior (1877) - *Exposição Succinta da Organisação actual da Universidade de Coimbra*. Imprensa da Universidade.

Viterbo, F. M. S. (1899) - *Diccionário histórico e documental dos architectos, engenheiros e constructores portugueses ou a serviço de Portugal*. Imprensa Nacional. I.

Wohl, H. (1973). Carlos Mardel and his Lisbon architecture. *Apollo* (Abril).

Wohl, H. (2000) - Robert C. Smith e a História da Arte nos Estados Unidos. In Jorge R. e Manuel C. (eds.). *Robert C. Smith (1912-1975). A investigação em história de arte*. Fundação Calouste Gulbenkian.

Sources

ARQUIVO DA UNIVERSIDADE DE COIMBRA (AUC). *Registo das Leis, Decretos, Portarias e Mais Artigos de Legislação Relativos Á Biblioteca da Universidade,* fl. 4 (AUC-IV-1.ª- E-1-2-7).

AUC. *Livro de Alvarás, Cartas e Provisões Régias*, Vol. 4 (1616-1746), fl. 43 (AUC, IV-1.ª- D-3-2-26).

AUC. *Biblioteca, Livro de Registo de Receita e Despesa de Obras*, Vol. I (1717) a Vol. 11 (1728) (AUC-IV- 1º - E-1-2-8 a 16).

AUC. *Construção da Biblioteca Joanina, Férias e Materiais* (1717-1728) (IV- 1.ª E-1-13 a IV- 1.ª- E-1-2-5).

AUC. *Construção da Biblioteca Joanina, Férias e Materiais* (1717-1718) (AUC-IV-1.ª-E - 1-1-13).

AUC. *Construção da Biblioteca Joanina, Férias e Materiais* (1717-1718) (AUC-IV-1.ª E-1-1-14).

AUC. *Construção da Biblioteca Joanina, Férias e Materiais* (1723-1724) (AUC-IV-1.ª E-1-2-1).

AUC. *Construção da Biblioteca Joanina, Obras*, Cx. 3 (1719) (AUC - IV- 1.ª E-1-1-15).

AUC. *Construção da Biblioteca Joanina, Obras*, Cx. 4 (1720-1722) (AUC-IV-1.ª E-1-1-16).

AUC. *Construção da Biblioteca Joanina, Obras*, Cx. 5 (1723-1724) (AUC-IV-1.ª E-1-2-1).

AUC. *Construção da Biblioteca Joanina, Obras*, Cx. 6 (1725-1726) (AUC-IV-1.ª E-1-2-2).

AUC. *Construção da Biblioteca Joanina, Obras*, Cx. 9 (1740-1743), fl. 4 de 1742 (AUC-IV, 1.ª E- 1-2-5).

AUC. *Livro de Receita e Despeza da Universidade*, Vol. 23 (1721-1724), fls. 80 v.º, de 1723. (AUC-IV-1.ª E-12-3-23).

AUC. *Livro de Receita e Despeza da Universidade*, Vol. 23 (1721-1724), fl. 88, de 1723 (AUC-IV-1.ª E-12-3-23).

AUC. *Livro da Receita e Despeza da Universidade*, Vol. 24 (1724-1728, fl. 81 de 1728 (AUC-IV-1.ª E-12-3-24).

AUC. *Livro de Receita e Despeza da Universidade*, Vol. 25 (1728-1732), fl. 79 v.º de 1729 e fl. 72 de 1730 (AUC-IV-1.ª E12-3-25).

AUC. *Livro de Receita e Despeza da Universidade*, Vol. 26 (1732-1736), fl. 39 de 1733 (AUC-IV-1.ª E-12-3-26).

AUC. *Livro de Receita e Despeza da Universidade*, vol. 26 (1732-1736), fl. 74 de 1733 (AUC-IV-1.ª E-12-3-26).

AUC. *Livro de Receita e Despeza da Universidade*, Vol. 28 (1740-1743) fl. 77 v.º de 1742. (AUC-IV-1.ª E- 12-3-28).

AUC. *Livro de Receita e Despeza*, Vol. 29 (1744-1747), fl. 78 de 1745 (AUC- IV-1.ª E-12-3-29).

AUC. *Livro da Receita e Despeza da Universidade*, Vol. 32 (1756-1759), fl. 78 v.º (1758) (AUC-IV-1.ª E-12-3-32).

AUC. *Universidade, Documentos de Despesas de Obras*, Cx. 3 (1796) (AUC- IV-1.ª E-10-1-3).

AUC. *Livro de Registo de Folhas Correntes de Obras*, Vol. 3, (1816-1818), fl. 88 (AUC-IV-1.ª E-10-2-21).

AUC. *Livro do Registo de Receita e Despesa das Obras* (1775-1776) (AUC-IV-1.ª E-10-2-31).

AUC. *Capela: Documentos avulsos* (AUC-IV-1.ª E-2-4-20).

AUC. *Documentos relativos a bens no bispado de Bragança* (Col) (IV-1.ª E-22-3-2).

AUC. *Fundo Notarial de Coimbra*. Tabelião Francisco Gomes Pinheiro. Dep.V; Sec.I-Es; Est.9; Tab.4; N.º.25, fls.15-16.

AUC. *Paróquia da Sé (Nova) de Coimbra*, B3 (1713-1741) (AUC-III-1.ª D-4-3).

AUC. *Paróquia de S. João da Cruz*, Livro de Óbitos, 1748-96, fl. 53 (1707-1795) (AUC III -2.ª-E-3-5).

AUC. *Tomo 2 dos Baptizados da Igreja do Real Mosteiro de Santa Cruz, 1626-1726,* livro 6, fl. 88-89.

AUC. Paróquia de Santa Cruz de Coimbra, *Livro dos Cazados de S. João de Sta. Cruz*, 1711-1768, fl. 43 (AUC, C2 (1711-1768) e (AUC-III-2.ª D-3-4).

AUC. Paróquia de Santa Cruz de Coimbra *Livro de Cazados de S. João de Santa Cruz,* 1711-1768, fl.118 (AUC, C2 (1711-1768) e (AUC-III-2.ª D-3-4).

AUC.Paróquia de Santa Cruz de Coimbra, *Livro de Óbitos de S. João de Santa Cruz,* fl. 106 v.º.

BIBLIOTECA GERAL DA UNIVERSIDADE DE COIMBRA. *Secção de Manuscritos*, "Provisões do Marques de Pombal e Plantas Referentes às Obras Projectadas por Ocasião da Reforma da Universidade de Coimbra em 1772", 3083- 3084.

ACADEMIA NACIONAL DE BELAS-ARTES. *fichas de sócios*. ficha de inscrição de Robert C. Smith.

ARQUIVO PESSOAL DO ARQUITETO NUNO TASSO DE SOUSA. *Cartas de Robert C. Smith.*

ASSOCIAÇÃO DOS ARQUEÓLOGOS PORTUGUESES. *fichas de sócios*, ficha de inscrição de Robert C. Smith.

BIBLIOTECA MUNICIPAL ROCHA PEIXOTO (BMRP). *Espólio Epistolográfico de Flávio Gonçalves. Cartas de Robert C. Smith.*

DIREÇÃO-GERAL DO PATRIMÓNIO CULTURAL - FORTE DE SACAVÉM. *DRMC-241-266.*

ESPÓLIO PROFISSIONAL DE EGÍDIO GUIMARÃES. *Epistolografia.*

FUNDAÇÃO CALOUSTE GULBENKIAN. *Espólio de Robert C. Smith.*

Web

ALMEIDA, Manuel Lopes de. 1900-1980, professor universitário e político. https://archeevo.amap.pt/details?id=75273

António José Teixeira, "Livraria da Universidade", *O Instituto*, 2nd series, vol. XXXVII, 1889-1890, pp. 305-312. https://digitalis-dsp.sib.uc.pt/institutocoimbra/UCBG-A-24-37a41_v037/UCBG-A-24-37a41_v037_item1/UCBG-A-24-37a41_v037.pdf.

"Antes e Depois | Sala do Senado (1867-2017)", *Boletim da Assembleia da República-Comunicar*, janeiro de 2017. https://app.parlamento.pt/comunicar/Artigo.aspx?ID=879

"Aspectos da Arquitectura Barroca Luso-Brasileira". https://gulbenkian.pt/historia-das-exposicoes/exhibitions/127/

Carlos Mardel. In *A Casa Senhorial entre Portugal, Brasil e Goa*. http://acasasenhorial.org/acs/index.php/pt/artistas/252-carlos-mardel-1695-1763.

Gravuras de Salomon Kleiner. https://www.gettyimages.com.br/fotos/salomon-kleiner

Gravuras de Paulo Decker. https://gallica.bnf.fr/ark:/12148/btv1b10501722r/f80.item.zoom.

Casa de Infância Doutor Elyseo de Moura. http://cidemoura.pt.

RAMALHO, Américo da Costa. https://www.uc.pt/bguc/destaques/AmericoCostaRamalho

Reitores dos séculos XVII a XIX. https://www.uc.pt/sobrenos/historia/reitores_xvii_xix

www.ingramcontent.com/pod-product-compliance
Lightning Source LLC
LaVergne TN
LVHW010353160826
845677LV00005BA/1267

9789892626321